Castle Cornet, Guernsey

CASTLES AND
OLD CHURCHES OF
THE CHANNEL ISLANDS

Mike Salter

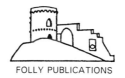

FOLLY PUBLICATIONS

ACKNOWLEDGEMENTS

The photographs in this book were taken by the author. who also prepared the plans, drawings, and maps. A few old postcards from the author's collection have also been reproduced. Plans of churches and chapels are all on a common scale of 1:400 and use a common system of hatching to show different periods of work, whilst the castle plans are on scales of 1:800 and 1:2000, except for that of Elizabeth Castle which has had to be reduced down to 1:4000 to squeeze it onto one page.

This book is dedicated to the men and women of Hurst Morris People (HuMP) of Berkshire with whom the author danced on Jersey in June 2000, and to whom he would like to say a big thank you for their help and support. Thanks are also due to Peter Halliwell of Wigmore in Herefordshire, who supplied the author with much useful material relating to the castles and forts described in this book.

ABOUT THIS BOOK

This book is the 43rd in a series describing castles and pre-19th century churches throughout all of Wales and Scotland and a considerable part of England. Normally the series (see list inside back cover) features different volumes for the castles and churches of each area. This volume, however, follows the format of the volume for the Isle of Man in that it includes parish churches and chapels dating up to the end of the 18th century, monastic buildings, and castles, forts and refuges dating up to the Civil War period of the mid 17th century.

ACCESS TO THE BUILDINGS

All the parish churches are accessible and they are generally kept open during the day. Some of the chapels lie on private land and permission to visit needs to be sought from the owners. Access to the priory ruins on Lihou island off the coast of Guernsey is only possible at low tide. La Hougue Bie, Elizabeth Castle and Mont Orgueil Castle on Jersey, and Castle Cornet on Guernsey are state monuments open to the public on payment of an admission fee. Elizabeth Castle is accessible on foot at low tide and when open by means of amphibious ferry vehicles at any state of the tide. The Chateau de Rocquaine on Guernsey contains a shipwreck museum for which an admission fee is payable. Les Cateaux and St Ouen's Manor on Jersey, the interior of St Aubin's Fort (located on a tidal island) and also the interior of Essex Castle on Alderney are private properties not normally open to the public. The other castles and forts described in this book are open spaces with unlimited access.

ABOUT THE AUTHOR

Mike Salter is 47 and has been a professional author and publisher since he went on the Government Enterprise Allowance Scheme for unemployed people in 1988. He is particularly interested in the planning and layout of medieval buildings and has a huge collection of plans of churches and castles he has measured during tours (mostly by bicycle and motorcycle) throughout all parts of the British Isles since 1968. Wolverhampton born and bred, Mike now lives in an old cottage beside the Malvern Hills. His other interests include walking, maps, railways, board games, morris dancing, playing percussion instruments and calling dances with a folk group.

Copyright 2001 by Mike Salter. First published March 2001
Folly Publications, Folly Cottage, 151 West Malvern Rd, Malvern, Worcs, WR14 4AY
Printed by Aspect Design, 89 Newtown Rd, Malvern, Worcs, WR14 2PD

St Martin's Church, Jersey

CONTENTS

Maps of buildings described appear inside the front cover.

HISTORICAL INTRODUCTION

The Channel Islands became part of the Duchy of Normandy in the 10th century. Duke William II took the Crown of England in 1066 but on his death on 1087 his eldest son Robert became Duke of Normandy and his second son became King William II of England. In the early 12th century, however, the youngest son, Henry took over both territories and since then the Channel Islands have been a possession of the English Crown, except for short-lived occupations by the French and Germans.

Alderney has a probable Roman fort called the Nunnery and there are several Iron Age promontory forts in Jersey and Guernsey. However, whilst the large but low moated mound of the Chateau des Marais on Guernsey is probably 12th century, serious fortification of the Channel Isles only became necessary after 1204. In that year King John lost all his possessions on the mainland of France to the French king, Philip Augustus. King John immediately began work on Castle Cornet in Guernsey and Mont Orgeuil Castle in Jersey. These castles had stone curtain walls flanked by towers and containing halls, chambers, chapels and outbuildings. They were supplemented by other strongpoints which do not seem to have been permanently occupied, and consequently had no domestic buildings of importance, but which could be used by the islanders as refuges during French raids. On Guernsey, in addition to the Chateau des Marais, the large Jerbourg Peninsular defended by a rampart, palisade and ditch was used as a strongpoint during the early 14th century, and there is a stone castle probably of the early 15th century at Vale. In the mid 14th century the vanished Tower of Beauregard was built on the south side of the town of St Peter Port, since although Castle Cornet protected the harbour it was too inaccessible for the townsfolk to flee into. On Jersey there is a stone courtyard castle at Grosnez and an earthwork of uncertain date and purpose at Les Cateaux, whilst on Alderney the Nunnery seems to have been refortified during the 15th century.

Vale Castle, Guernsey

Gunner's Tower, Castle Cornet

Inside the hall block at Mont Orgueil Castle

In 1275 Edward made Otto de Grandison, son of a baron of Savoy, Warden of the Channel Isles, a position he held until his death in 1328. He was also Seneschal of Gascony and only rarely visited the isles, which were ruled by lieutenants. The French invaded Guernsey in 1294 and 1338, Castle Cornet being captured on the latter occasion. They tried to occupy Jersey but Mont Orgeuil Castle held out against them. The English retook Guernsey in 1340 after defeating the French fleet at the Battle of Sluys, but only recovered Castle Cornet in 1345, Jerbourg being used as the seat of government for Guernsey in the meantime. Edward III subsequently invaded the mainland of France and the danger of French invasions of the Channel Isles receded for the moment. In 1483 a bull of Pope Sixtus IV confirmed an agreement between the kings of England and France for the Channel Islands to be regarded as neutral.

Henry VIII's break with the Roman Catholic Church in the 1530s left the islands open to invasion again. Consequently both Castle Cornet and Mont Orgueil were refortified for defence by and against cannon. New forts were also built on Alderney and on a rock in St Aubin's Bay on Jersey. Mont Orgueil was considered to be vulnerable to bombardment on the landward side and although like Castle Cornet it continued in use up until the end of World War II, it was eventually superseded by Elizabeth Castle, which is set on a tidal island guarding Jersey's principal harbour of St Helier. Begun in a modest fashion as a battery on a rock during Elizabeth's reign, this fortress attained its present spacious layout under Charles II in the 1670s. Vale Castle on Guernsey was rebuilt in the 17th century, and perhaps also the medieval or Tudor stronghold which stood on the site of the present Fort Grey on Guernsey, but the other refuge strongholds do not seem to have then been in use.

The many towers and forts built in the Channel Isles from the late 18th century onwards do not form part of the scope of this book, which is essentially about buildings from the medieval, Tudor and Stuart periods of British history.

THE DEVELOPMENT OF THE CHURCHES

Several of the medieval parish churches of Guernsey and Jersey are known to have existed by the mid 11th century. The division of Guernsey into ten parishes and Jersey into twelve parishes is assumed to go back to at least as early as then. One church on Guernsey is dedicated to St Sampson, who is reputed to have introduced Christianity to the island, and who died c565. By that time a bishopric had been established at Coutances on the French mainland only 30km SE of Jersey. The Channel Islands formed part of that bishopric until 1569, when they were transferred to that of Winchester. A monastery on Sark was founded by St Maglorious (a kinsman of St Sampson), who died c586, and excavations have revealed traces of an early hermitage on the Ile Agois, off the coast of Jersey. In 1976 a celtic cross probably of the 8th century was found in the parish of St Peter's on Guernsey, and a church is thought to have existed at Vale in that period, whilst on Jersey a church may have stood at St Lawrence's by the early seventh century.

The first churches in the Channel Islands may have been of wood or drystone construction. None of the existing churches contain any structural work likely to predate the early 12th century, by which time the dukes of Normandy (which included the Channel Islands) were also kings of England. Of that period are the naves at Castel on Guernsey and St Clement's on Jersey, The Fishermen's Chapel at St Brelade's on Jersey is also probably of that period. Originally these churches would have consisted of just a nave to accommodate a standing congregation (seats were only introduced much later) and a small square chancel or simple semi-circular apse to contain the altar. The interiors would have been dark since these churches only had a few narrow round-headed windows and probably only a single doorway.

St Lawrence's Church, Jersey

North chapel at Vale, Guernsey

The period 1140-1200 was a busy one for the construction or extension of churches in the Channel Islands. All twelve of the medieval churches on Jersey and five of those on Guernsey have work of that period. The churches on Jersey all had their original small chancels replaced by central towers, beyond which longer new chancels were provided. Most of these towers still survive, although some of them have had their upper parts rebuilt later, and two (St Helier and St Saviour) were entirely rebuilt later in the medieval period. The spires with lucarnes or tall narrow loops and spirelets at the corners on several Jersey churches are probably late 14th or 15th century, but precise dating is difficult, especially as some have been concreted over to make them waterproof. On Guernsey only Castel still has a 12th century central tower, those at St Sampson and St Saviour having been replaced by other towers located elsewhere, whilst at Vale a new nave was added to a rib-vaulted chancel of c1140, and a tower was then built at the west end of the nave.

St Ouen's Church, Jersey

On Guernsey the plan form of a central tower located between the nave and chancel was adopted in the 13th century churches of Forest and St Martin's, and also appears at St Peter Port, where the earliest parts are 13th century, although the central tower itself is 15th century. St Sampson has a 13th century north transeptal tower as does the small church that served Lihou Priory. Transepts were added on either side of the central towers at many churches during the 13th century, Castel and St Saviour's on Guernsey each still having one remaining, whilst on Jersey St Brelade's, St Clement's and St Peter's each have two, whilst at St Helier's and St Lawrence's only one has survived subsequent rebuilding and alterations. The transepts contained extra altars, as did the chapels added on the north side of the chancels at St Helier's, St Lawrence's, St Peter's and Trinity on Jersey and St Sampson's and Vale on Guernsey. Vale also has a north aisle to the nave of this period. Another once existed at Torteval, the only medieval church in the Channel Islands which has been totally destroyed and replaced by a 19th

St Peter's Church, Jersey

century building. The church at St Peter Port has a rather short nave because it occupies a cramped site within a town (it is usually referred to as Town Church) and consequently it appears to have already possessed an aisle on each side by the end of the 13th century. On Guernsey St Pierre du Bois and Castel each gained a south aisle in the 14th century but it does not appear that any of the churches on Jersey possessed an aisle beside the full length of the nave before the 15th century.

Churches in the Channel Islands are characterised by having pointed vaults throughout as is common in Normandy. Vaults were not normally provided in the 12th century, yet by the mid 13th century most of the churches had been given them. The vaults are usually divided into bays by strips called doubleux which when vaults first started to be built continued from internal pilaster buttresses but later on were corbelled out at the level of springing of the vaults. External pilaster buttresses remained the norm in the Channel Islands until the end of the 14th century. Commonly the doubleaux divide chancels into two bays and naves into three bays. Chapels may have a single doubleaux but the later medieval aisles often lack them.

The arcades of the aisles at St Peter Port are early 14th century. Otherwise work of that period in the churches mostly takes the form of chapels beside the chancel. There are 14th century north chapels at St Brelade's and St Clement's on Jersey, whilst the south chapels of St Sampson's on Guernsey and Grouville on Jersey extend further west to absorb the former south transepts. The chapels on each side of the church at St Ouen not only replaced the transepts but extended one more bay to flank the east part of the nave. The south chapel is late 13th century and the north chapel is 14th century. The south chapel of c1390 at St Martin's is the earliest building on Jersey to feature diagonal corner buttresses. They appear on several 16th century aisles on Jersey and also on two 15th century towers on Guernsey. At Castel on Guernsey the 14th century south aisle and south chapel have now become the nave and chancel since the modern congregation expects a better view of the priest's activities in the chancel than is allowed by the arches under the tower. The chapel (probably of c1370) slightly predates the aisle and has the earliest instance in the Channel Islands of walling formed of roughly shaped blocks called moellons instead of the rough rubble used previously. Vaults remained the norm throughout the late medieval period, especially on Jersey, but the later vaults sometimes lack doubleux.

Gradually more space was required for congregations and aisles were added on. On Jersey the churches of St Helier and St Martin were each given a south aisle in the 15th century, whilst in the 16th century St Brelade's, St John's, St Lawrence's and St Saviour's were each given a north aisle, St Peter's was given a south aisle and St Ouen's was given an aisle on each side, the only instance of this on Jersey up until St Peter's was given a second aisle on the north side in the 19th century. At St Lawrence's the additional work also included a larger new north transept and a north chapel, both of which are rib-vaulted. At St Saviour's the tower and south transept were rebuilt in the 15th century. Grouville has a north chapel which extends further west to replace the former transept, whilst St Martin has a north transeptal chapel is an amalgam of late medieval and post-Reformation period work. On Guernsey both St Andrew's and St Saviour's have 15th century north aisles which extend to the east end to provide chapels. Each aisle ends at the west end in a tower with a rib-vault inside. The lost church of Torteval also had a tower in such a NW corner position, but it was of earlier date. Forest also has a north aisle extending further east to form a chapel. Much of the church at St Peter Port is 15th century, with a rib-vaulted central tower and a chancel flanked by north and south chapels. These chapels have arcades with hollow chamfers on the arches. Since the short nave and aisle did not allow enough space for the congregation further space was created by building an extended south transept with an aisle on its east side. Most of the church at St Pierre du Bois is 15th century work. This is the only church on Guernsey apart from that at St Peter Port to have both north and south aisles. The tower here, along plus the much earlier one at Vale, are the only medieval examples in the Channel Islands lying at the west end of a nave, by far the most common position for a tower in English parish churches. As in the 15th century parts of the church at St Peter Port St Pierre du Bois has no vaulting. Alone amongst the Channel Island churches it resembles churches in Cornwall, where again granite is the normal building material.

St John's Church, Jersey

The 15th century tower at St Pierre du Bois is unusual in having a contemporary porch set on the north side of it. Amongst Guernsey churches there are other 15th century porches at St Peter Port and Vale, 14th century porches at Castel and St Saviour's and a 16th century porch at St Martin's. The porch at Castel lies at the west end of the nave, as do three examples on Jersey, those of the 15th century at Grouville and St Brelade's, and a 14th century porch at St Martin's on Jersey. A 15th century porch on the north side of the nave at St Helier has been mostly rebuilt. The Jersey churches lack separate vestries but on Guernsey there are 16th century examples at St Sampson's, St Saviour's and Vale, and 19th century examples at Forest and St Helier. In modern times vestries have now been partitioned off within other churches, as in the aisle at St Martin's on Guernsey.

All the churches were restored during the 19th century, quite a number of windows being replaced and the upper parts of towers and spires rebuilt because of storm damage. On Guernsey the only really major works to the medieval churches since 1600 have been the rebuilding in the 18th century of the 16th century north aisle and chapel at St Martin's and the addition of a large new vestry at St Helier. To these should be added the entirely new early 19th century church replacing the destroyed medieval one at Torteval and the new Trinity church at St Peter Port, a classical style building of 1789 containing box pews. Guernsey also has seven 19th century churches, most of them in and around St Peter Port. One of them is a Catholic church, as are the church of Our Lady, dating from 1961 and the celebrated tiny chapel of Les Vaubelets dating from the 1920s. On Jersey the churches of St Mary and St Peter have 19th century aisles, Trinity has a completely new nave, and St Helier has a west extension to the nave and a new south transept beyond where the original one (swallowed up by a late medieval aisle and chapel) once lay. There are about a dozen 19th century churches on Jersey, two thirds of them being in and around St Helier. That at St Aubin's is a replacement of a destroyed 18th century church. There are also several 20th century places of worship on Jersey. The churches on Alderney and Sark are both 19th century buildings, although the former retains an 18th century tower added to the vanished medieval building.

On the whole the churches of the Channel Isles tend to be rather plain. Doorways lack the nook-shafts common in English 12th and 13th centuriy churches, nor are there carvings of figures or animals. Only the 15th and 16th century doorways have much in the way of decoration, with roll-mouldings or floriated hood-moulds. Early windows are simple and there are no examples of the type of long, narrow, pointed lancet common in 13th century buildings in England and Wales. Large windows with complex tracery forms only became common from the 1440s onwards and then are mostly confined to end gables, the chancels and chapels of Jersey churches having a fine series of east windows with up to four lights with Flamboyant tracery utilising the ogival arch. However, there is nothing in any of the churches to compare with the large flat-arched or straight-headed windows found in the side walls of many 15th century English churches, windows on the north and south sides of Channel Island churches rarely having more than two lights. On Guernsey the only window with as many as four lights is the end window of the south transept at St Peter Port.

At the Reformation of the mid 16th century the islands adopted a Presbyterian form of church government which lasted in Jersey until 1623 and in Guernsey until 1663. The churches were scraped clean of all images and anything else that smacked of Catholicism. Consequently they contain very few furnishings or monuments older than the 18th century. Until the Reformation the interiors were a riot of colour. Wall paintings of saints were then scraped off or covered with whitewash, and stained glass effigies were replaced by plain glass. Wall paintings do survive on Jersey at Grouville, St Clement's, and in the Fishermen's Chapel at St Brelades, whilst on Guernsey there are traces of paintings at Castel and in the late 14th century chapel of St Appoline in the parish of St Saviour. Also removed were the screens that originally closed off the west ends of chancels. In England screens often carried lofts used by musicians and upon which were mounted images of the Crucifixion, something that was particularly objectionable to the reformers. None of the Channel Islands churches retain any access steps to lofts, except that at St Brelade's a loft was reached by means of the central tower staircase. Even fonts were removed and the only medieval ones surviving are 15th century examples at Grouville (a rare double one) and St Clement's on Jersey and St Martin's on Guernsey. On the other hand medieval piscinas are common enough. Many of them are 15th and 16th century examples with ogival heads with foliated hoodmoulds but a much plainer double piscina of the 13th century remains at St Brelade's on Jersey. There are also several ornate late medieval recesses containing credence shelves and a few decorated brackets which once supported images.

Tombs also suffered and no medieval ones remain, although there is a small niche containing two early 16th century figures on the outside of the south chapel at St Martin's on Jersey and there are a few medieval cross-slabs. Indents of lost 15th century brasses depicting civilians and their wives remain at the Guernsey churches of St Peter Port and Vale. There is also an indent of a 16th century single figure at St Saviour's. Another recorded indent at St Martin's is no longer visible.

FURTHER READING

Buildings and Memorials of The Channel Islands, Raoul Lempriere, 1980
Channel Island Churches, John McCormack, 1986
Societe Jersiaise Annual Bulletin.
Transactions of La Societe Guernesiaise
Guide pamphlets are available for Castle Cornet on Guernsey and for Elizabeth Castle, Mont Orgueil Castle and La Hougue Bie on Jersey.
Several of the parish churches also have pamphlet guides available.

CASTLES OF GUERNSEY

BEAUREGARD TOWER

This fortress is said to have been erected by Edward III in 1357 to act as a refuge for the townsfolk of St Peter Port. The king permitted the town to be walled in 1350 but if work on such walls was ever begun the circuit was never completed. There are no remains of defences on the mainland here, either of town walls or of Beauregard Tower, which seems to have included a defensible courtyard as well as a tower. It stood on Tower Hill at the south end of the town. Excavations found traces of a ditch in Cliff Street (formerly La Coupee de La Tour Beauregard). Pottery fragment indicated the ditch was already silting up by the 1380s. There was also another tower called La Tour Grand near the Plaiderie, although the exact site is uncertain.

CASTLE CORNET

This castle lies on an island near the entrance to St Peter Port Harbour and is now connected to the mainland by a long quay erected in the 1860s. Previously access was probably by a causeway. The castle is assumed to have been founded by King John after the loss of Normandy, and is presumed to be "the King's Castle at Guernsey" to which a supply of "bretasches" was despatched from Seaford in Sussex in 1206. Bretasches can mean either palisading or the hoarding used as a timber form of machicolation at a wall-head. In this case it probably means the latter, since such a rocky site unsuited to the digging of earthworks and raising of palisades must surely have had a stone curtain wall from the start. The castle once had a circular tower keep, either as an original feature or as an addition by Henry III in the 1220s or 30s. In 1244 King Henry ordered Drew de Barentin to repair the west wall of the castle and roof with lead two old towers plus six new towers, and a barbican was to be provided. In 1252 de Barentin was given instructions to repair storm damage to the tower (presumably the keep), "the chapel and other houses damaged by the wind, as well as the wall of the castle".

Castle Cornet from the quay

Entrance passage at Castle Cornet   *The gateway at Castle Cornet*

In 1294 the French invaded Guernsey but Castle Cornet, which had been substantially repaired two years earlier, was not captured. In 1328 the new Warden of the Channel Isles, John de Roche, found that Castle Cornet had a garrison of six men-at-arms and fifty archers, for whom he ordered a supply of crossbows and shields. Repairs carried out in the early 1330s included work upon a tower called "La Mangonel", which presumably had a catapult of that type mounted on its roof. The French raided Southampton in 1338 and twice invaded the Channel Islands, capturing Castle Cornet in September of that year. Warden Thomas de Ferrers' lieutenant Walter de Weston managed to recapture Guernsey in 1340 but a truce was made with the French before Castle Cornet could be taken. The castle was closely besieged by the English for three months during the summer of 1342, thirty-one seamen being employed in a barge to encircle the castle and prevent supplies getting through. However, the French garrison in the castle held out, another truce was made in 1343, and Castle Cornet only finally fell to the English when hostilities broke out again in 1345 and it was closely invested for three days by a large force under Godfrey d'Harcourt and then stormed with the aid of scaling ladders.

In later years the castle was normally garrisoned by fourteen men in addition to the the lieutenant, the marshal, the porter, the sutler (in charge of provisions), the master gunner, the smith, the carpenter, and a number of boatmen and watchmen, but it was doubled in time of war. The lieutenant was empowered to commandeer suitable men from the rest of the island for the defence of the castle, and all those with carts or boats were obliged to give two days service towards carrying materials for building work when required. Each year the garrison were supplied with 100 hogsheads of beer or quantities of malt and hops, 12 beef carcases, 600 flitches of bacon, 3000 stockfish, quantities of butter and cheese, 300lb of tallow, and leather, wood and coal. In the 1430s work at the castle included the erection of a new tower, probably the still surviving Gunners' Tower.

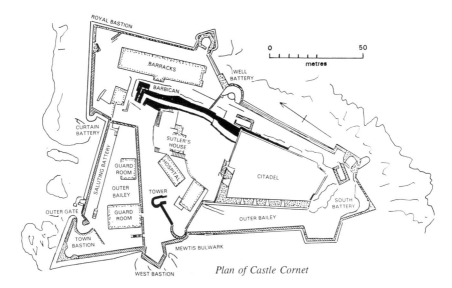

Plan of Castle Cornet

In the 1530s the castle defences began to be updated for defence by artillery and the Mewtis and Well batteries are that period. The western defences are thought to have been improved by Sir Frances Chamberlayne between 1567 and 1570 in response to the threat of bombardment from a new pier on the site of the present Albert Pier. During the first half of the governorship of Sir Thomas Leighton from 1570 to 1609 the existing outer line of defence with its several batteries and bastions was built, these works being shown complete on a view of the castle made in 1593. On the north side a new wall was later erected to create an intermediate line of defence should the main gateway in the Town Bastion be forced by attackers. This work may date from the period 1643 to 1651 when Castle Cornet held a garrison commanded by the Governor Sir Peter Osborne, although the rest of Guernsey supported Parliament. The defenders constantly harassed St Peter Port with their gunfire but guns on the shore managed to open up a breach somewhere on the west side. In March 1651 an attempt was made to storm the castle but it was repulsed and many of the attackers were left stranded on the rocks outside the castle walls. The defeat of Charles II at the Battle of Worcester in September was a severe setback for the Royalist cause and a fleet under Admiral Blake captured the Scilly Isles and Jersey. In the middle of December Colonel Burgess, who had replaced Sir Peter Osborne, surrendered Castle Cornet on favourable terms which allowed his men to leave complete with all their equipment.

In 1662 the restored Charles II appointed Lord Hatton as Governor. He was succeeded by his son the 2nd Lord Hatton in 1670. During a great storm in December 1672 a bolt of lightning managed to penetrate the keep, which was used as a powder magazine. The resulting explosion completely destroyed the keep and all of the adjacent apartments, which had recently been refurbished. Seven people were killed, including the Governor's wife, mother and steward. Two of his children survived the demolition of the nursery in which two maids died, and the Governor himself survived being blown out of his newly erected apartment, which stood NE of the keep. The central parts of the castle were still in a wrecked state when Colonel Legge reported on the state of the island's defences to Charles II in 1680. The report estimated that repairs would cost over £16,700.

In the mid 18th century new buildings to accommodate the garrison were provided and eventually the south bailey was filled with soil and rubble to make an elevated artillery platform known as the citadel. During the Napoleonic wars the castle was armed with over seventy guns. A second guard room was added during the Victorian period. Later buildings have now mostly been demolished, although there are a few traces of the modifications made by the Germans in the 1940s. In 1947 King George VI handed over the castle to the people of Guernsey for preservation as an ancient monument.

The combined effects of the explosion which destroyed the keep and the inner court with its buildings, and the conversion of the southern bailey into an artillery citadel have not left much of the medieval castle still standing. No traces remains of the keep or of the medieval and 17th century apartments. Old illustrations show the lofty circular keep standing on a boss of rock and having a semi-circular stair turret on the west side. A little of the masonry revetment of the citadel is 13th century lower down, and near the NE corner are three shallow buttresses of that date almost hidden by an adjacent 17th century magazine. Under the battery on the citadel roof are 19th century casemates which are not open to the public. A rectangular projection at the citadel south end marks the site of the Tour Carre, from which in 1643 the three Parliamentary island commissioners James de Havilland, Peter Carey and Peter de Beauvoir, who had been captured by the castle garrison, escaped after forty-three days imprisonment, during which they made a rope of flax.

The inner ward wall at Castle Cornet

The Saluting Battery and outer ward at Castle Cornet

The Hart Bulwark at Castle Cornet   *The medieval entrance passage*

On the east side of the inner bailey there survives a long entrance passage from the outer gate (with a slot above for the hoist of a former drawbridge) under the mostly rebuilt Prison Tower to the inner gate near the SE corner, near which is a postern leading out towards the 16th century Well Battery of the outer defences. Originally a secure covered way led from the postern to the water supply. In later years the former entrance passage was used as a secure exercise yard for prisoners kept in the Prison Tower. The barbican containing a right-angled outer extension (with portcullis groove) of the main entrance passage is thought to be a relic of the French occupation of the 1340s but the machicolated tower adjoining it probably dates from the 1430s. There are also corbels for machicolations on the contemporary U-shaped Gunners' Tower, a building 6m in diameter externally probably standing on the site of a 13th century tower. The lowest of its three levels has a later brick vault and two gunports, one facing north which is now blocked and another facing west which was widened later. No trace remains of the 45m long length of curtain wall which once ran from it to the Prison Tower. South of where this lost curtain lay is the Hospital, which is dated 1746 on the doorway lintel. East of it stands the Sutler's House, a building of 1600 which was low down enough to escape the worst of the 1672 explosion, although all its features are of later date. South of the Gunner's Tower is a store under which descends a passage down to the western part of the outer ward. Just 10m north of the lost curtain wall is a high retaining wall built in the mid 17th century to provide an intermediate line of defence, although the brick parapet is later. Over the angled entrance through this wall, where it meets the outer line of defence are the arms of Elizabeth II, commemorating a royal visit in 1957. Above this gateway is a small garden which was cultivated by General Sir John Lambert, a Parliamentarian kept prisoner in the castle by Charles II from 1660 to 1670. Here he cultivated the Guernsey Lily, now the floral symbol of the island.

The Mewtis Bulwark at the western corner of the inner ward has a 16th century battery with three gunports set on an older base. This is the only part of the two medieval baileys not to be surrounded by the late 16th century outer defences which lie at a lower level. The bastions are all carefully laid out to cover each other and not leave any blind corners unflanked. On the north side they have orillons or rounded projections covering the batteries in their flanks. The outer gate lies in the east flank of the Town Bastion at the NW corner and was thus protected from bombardment from the mainland. Over the gateway are the arms of Elizabeth I and above are two original gunports. The outer parts of this bastion were damaged during the Civil War and has seen much later rebuilding. From it the outer wall runs south to the West Bastion, which is commanded by the nearby Mewtis Bastion. The entrance passage (closed by a portcullis) curves round under the bastion and comes out in the outer ward facing a mid 18th century guard room. The north curtain commands the harbour and has a saluting battery on top. It runs east to the Curtain Battery, from which a gun dated 1799 with the cypher of George III is fired at noon every day. This battery lies in the west flank of the bastion known as the Royal Battery. South of here and east of the barbican is a barrack block intended to accommodate married soldiers. It is dated 1745 on the NE corner and 1750 on the rain-water heads, and now contains a museum. The outer wall runs south behind the barracks to the ivy-leaf-shaped Hart Bulwark, projecting dramatically to command the whole seaward side of the castle. The wall then runs SW to the Well Battery and a 55m long section of wall reaches to the easternmost of a triple series of three batteries at the south end of the outer ward. The basic shape of this preserves the 16th century layout but there has been much remodelling and rebuilding. There is also another 17th century magazine here. Like its twin close to the Well Battery it has an 18th century brick vault.

The barbican at Castle Cornet

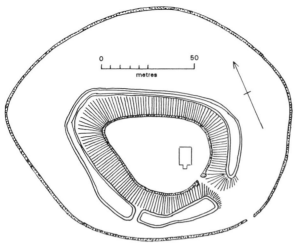

Plan of the Chateau des Marais

The barbican at Castle Cornet

CHATEAU DES MARAIS (IVY CASTLE)

Just inland from Belle Grebe Bay is a mound surrounded by a wet moat crossed by a causeway at the SE end. The egg-shaped summit 60m long by 40m wide is enclosed by a low wall with two slight solid round projections flanking the gateway. This wall was mostly rebuilt in the 18th century, when a magazine was built near the SE end, and is no more than a breastwork. The same is true of an outer wall enclosing a surrounding bailey 150m by 125m which largely relied on the former surrounding marsh for its protection. Excavations in 1975-7 revealed footings of buildings on the summit of the mound. The castle is thought to have been erected in the 12th century to serve as a refuge. There is circumstantial evidence of it existing in 1195, the site then being called Marais d' Orgeuil, not to be confused with Mont Orgeuil Castle on Jersey. The castle chapel, dedicated to St Mary, or its chaplains are mentioned in 1262, 1328, 1331 and 1382 and fields belonging to the then probably long abandoned building are mentioned in 1573 and 1616. The castle site was occupied by the Germans in the 1940s and contains a bunker of that period.

Chateau des Marais

Fort Grey on the site of the Chateau de Rocquaine

CHATEAU DE ROCQUAINE (FORT GREY)

A causeway leads across the beach of Rocquaine Bay on the SW side of Guernsey to a rock on which stands a martello tower of 1804 surrounded by a breastwork outer wall with eight embrasures for cannon and an entrance at the foot of a flight of steps on the east side. The tower of this structure, known as Fort Grey, now forms a shipwreck museum. A report by Colonel Legge to Charles II made in 1680 shows this site as occupied by a structure with a court of similar size entered from the north and having a rectangular building in the middle, whilst the east side was shielded from bombardment from the mainland by a higher section of rampart with a round tower or turret at each end. A water colour of 1775 by Captain Francis Cross also shows a castle-like structure on the site, and it is also shown on "A New Chart" on display in the museum.

THE JERBOURG PENINSULAR

This peninsular at the island SE corner has a nearly flat top 600m wide and 1,100m long with precipitous cliffs on all sides except to the north where the 400m long neck is closed off by a rampart and ditch of Neolithic or early Bronze Age date, although refortified many times. Other ramparts close off the smaller headlands of Jerbourg Point and St Martin's Point. After Castle Cornet was captured by the French in the 1320s the English Crown used the Jerbourg peninsular as an alternative seat of government for Guernsey. In any case Castle Cornet's island location made it unsuitable as a refuge for the people of Guernsey. There seems to have been a square stone tower somewhere behind this outer line of defence. A constable and six archers constituted the permanent garrison in 1337. The fortress was captured by the French in 1338, but was recaptured by the English in 1340 and strengthened. The defences are referred to as destroyed in 1350, perhaps having been dismantled after the English recovered Castle Cornet, but the site seems to have seen further use as a refuge later on and the Germans strengthened the landward defences in the 1940s.

Vale Castle

VALE CASTLE

The largest portion of the parish of Vale formed a separate island until in 1806 the tidal Braye de Valle was enclosed as part of the defensive provisions made against Napoleon. The castle stands on a rock facing east and seems to have served as the island refuge. Probably of 15th century origin and originally without any permanent internal buildings, it was remodelled in the 17th and late 18th centuries, barracks (now removed) were added in the 19th century and further modifications were made by the Germans in the 1940s. A wall about 1.2m thick encloses a D-shaped court about 60m by 40m. The straight back of the D actually curves slightly inwards and has at one end a gateway facing south. D-shaped towers about 5m across flank the wall, three of them around the north and north-west sides, another at the south corner and a fifth close to it facing SW. A rampart of earth with a stone face towards the court backs the outer wall except on the north and NE sides.

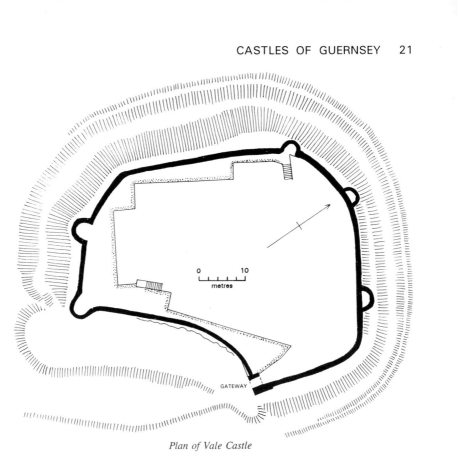

Plan of Vale Castle

The SE front and gateway at Vale Castle

OLD PARISH CHURCHES OF GUERNSEY

CASTEL - St Mary

This church commands an extensive view to the north and is said to be on the site of a fortress, although there has been a church here since at least the 1150s. The original chancel (now a north chapel) contains 13th century wall paintings depicting the Three Living and the Three Dead, and the Last Supper. This part, buttressed in three bays but with the vault divided only into two, is late 12th century, as are the massive crossing piers under the tower. Towards the end of that period the older nave (now the north aisle) was provided with a vault and pilaster buttresses. The north transept is early 13th century. In the late 14th century the south transept was replaced by a wide chapel extended as far east as the chancel, and then a few years later this was extended westwards to form an aisle with one wide arch to the western half of the nave but two narrower arches with an octagonal pier towards the nave eastern part. The aisle and chapel now serve as the nave and chancel. One south window is late 15th century and two windows further west are 17th or 18th century, whilst the west doorway of the aisle now used as a nave is 15th century. The west doorway of the original nave has a late 14th century porch in front of it. A narrow squint has been channelled through the SE pier of the tower.

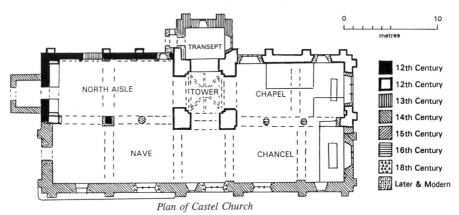

Plan of Castel Church

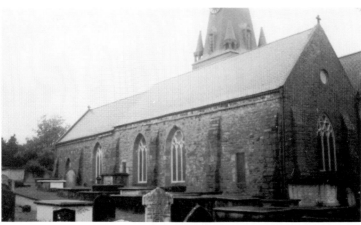

Castel Church

Forest Church

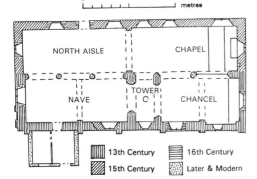

Plan of Forest Church

Interior of Forest Church

FOREST - St Margaret

This is the smallest medieval church on Guernsey. In the 15th century a north aisle was built alongside the entire length of a 13th century church consisting of a nave and chancel, each vaulted in two bays, with a tower raised over a narrow crossing between them. A church here existed by the mid 11th century. The aisle vault has just one dividing pilaster, level with the west arch of the crossing. The aisle has some original windows, but it has an early 16th century east window (and an adjacent piscina) and the round-headed doorway and two windows further west are late 16th century. The chancel and crossing each have one original window, and the nave has an original south doorway now opening into a modern building forming a porch with a vestry on the west side. Two other south windows are of the 15th and 16th centuries respectively. The tower has an octagonal spire and four corner spirelets and contains a clock commemorating Queen Victoria's Jubilee in 1897. The north aisle now serves as the nave and chancel and contains a poorbox of oak bound with iron and a collection of wind instruments used by the church band before an organ was built in the SE corner of the original chancel. The granite font under the tower is of 1968. There is much stained glass and the chancel has a tablet to Edouart Mourant, d1836, who was Rector of Forest and Torteval for thirty-nine years.

St Andrew's Church   *The porch at St Martin's Church*

ST ANDREW

The nave and slightly wider chancel, both with several pilaster buttresses, and traces of two original windows, are late 12th century, but the vaults are probably mid 13th century. The recesses the chancel are probably 14th century. In the mid 15th century the church was provided with a new west wall containing a doorway and an aisle was added with a tower at the west end projecting beyond the nave west end. The tower has a rib-vault and an embattled parapet around the base of a slate-covered spire with a weathercock. The aisle has several old windows but parts of the arcade and all of the south windows are post-1800. The oldest memorials are those to Jean Guille of Rohais, d1758, and Charles Antoine Frederic Gounon de Predon, d1778.

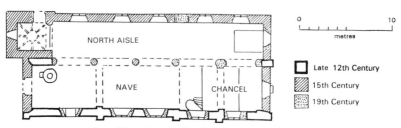

NORTH AISLE

NAVE   CHANCEL

0   10
metres

☐ Late 12th Century

▨ 15th Century

▨ 19th Century

Plan of St Andrew's Church

ST MARTIN

The 13th century nave and chancel have set-back pilaster angle buttresses and are vaulted in two bays. Between them is a narrow rib-vaulted crossing with an iron spiral stair up to a tower covered by an octagonal granite spire with corner spirelets. The south windows are late 16th century, and the east window and piscina are late 15th century, so the only 13th century feature is the south doorway, beside which are the oak cupboard poor box set into a former stoup, and the medieval font, restored to the church in 1869, having previously been removed. In front of the doorway is an early 16th century Flamboyant style porch with diagonal buttresses with crocketted pinnacles. The 18th century north aisle vaulted in six bays replaces a 16th century aisle, of which the arcades remain, and contains the pulpit, dated 1657. The west bay (in which is a reset early 14th century doorway) is screened off to serve as a vestry. The best of several tablets to members of the families of Andros, Carey, de Sausmarez, and Gosselin, is that under the tower to Amice Andros, Seigneur of Sausmarez and Bailiff of Guernsey, d1674, with his wife Elizabeth Stone. A rectangular pillar gatepost between two gates on the south side of the churchyard is carved with a female head and shoulders, probably of sixth century date. There are several 20th century stained glass window memorials.

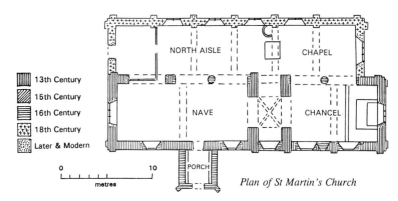

13th Century
15th Century
16th Century
18th Century
Later & Modern

NORTH AISLE

CHAPEL

NAVE

CHANCEL

PORCH

0   10
metres

Plan of St Martin's Church

St Martin's Church

ST PETER PORT - Town Church (St Peter)

There is no graveyard, and the building is surrounded by public thoroughfares. Until demolished in 1787 there was a vaulted charnel house south of the church, originally the chapel of St Sepulchre or its undercroft, and later used as a military stores. As a result of being so hemmed in the church is shorter than one might otherwise expect for such an important building, with a nave and chancel each only two bays long on either side of an early 15th century central tower set upon substantial piers with a rib-vaulted crossing. There is, however, a substantial south transept three bays long with an east aisle containing a piscina. This part is late 15th century (it bears the date 1466), as indeed is most of the exterior, when the chancel east wall, the north transept end wall, and north and south chapel outer walls were rebuilt, a small north porch added beside the transept, the nave and south aisle west walls were refaced, and a turret provided in the angle between the south aisle and south transept to contain a stair to the tower upper parts. The tower contains an 18th century clock and the lead covered spire is dated 1721 with an inscription and the keys of St Peter. The porch has two carved rabbits and an upper room reached by a spiral staircase. There is a heads on the outside SE corner of the south transept and another on the north chapel NE corner. The oldest parts of the building are the 13th century aisles on either side of a nave which was rebuilt in the early 14th century, the arches here springing from only just above ground level, in contrast to the early 15th century arcades further east with short octagonal piers.

Memorials in the nave and aisles include those of Captain William Sheldon, d1680, Captain Nicholas Le Messurier, d1759, and John Fiott, d1761. The north chapel formerly had an ecclesiastical court divided off in the upper part of it and contains memorials to Josue la Marchant, d1795, and to William Marchant and his family (early 19th century). Originally the Lady Chapel, and having a fine piscina with an ogival head with finials, this part of the church is now called the Brock Memorial Chapel and has a screen which commemorates Major-General Sir Isaac Brock, famous for his campaign in Canada in 1812. There are many other memorials on the south transept west wall. East of the transept are spacious modern vestries. Several flags hang in the church and there are many stained glass memorial windows, some of them replacements of windows wrecked during the German Occupation.

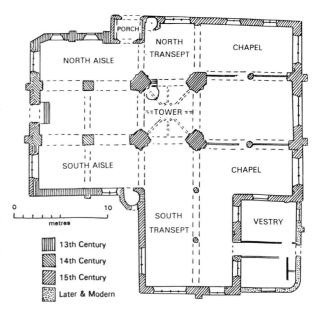

Plan of Town Church, St Peter Port

Trinity Church at St Peter Port   *Town Church, St Peter Port*

ST PETER PORT - Trinity Church

The growth of St Peter Port eventually necessitated the building of a second church in Trinity Square in 1789. It is a classical style building with Dutch gables, and stuccoed walls, but with dressings and quoins of granite. It consists of a vestibule and a main body with a gallery. There a box pews, two fonts, a brass lectern and a pulpit carved with the story of the prodigal son.

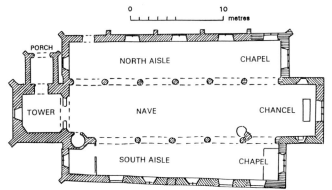

Plan of St Pierre du Bois Church

Porch Doorway at Town Church

St Pierre du Bois Church

ST PIERRE DU BOIS

Most of this church dates from the last quarter of the 15th century. It is built against a slope and the floor consequently rises quite noticeably towards the east. The layout recalls the churches of Devon and Cornwall. It comprises an undivided nave and chancel with wooden-roofed aisles, almost semi-circular arcade arches upon octagonal piers, and a 34m high embattled and diagonally buttressed west tower. The tower has the very unusual feature of a diagonally buttressed porch set on its north side, whilst the tower staircase is contained in a turret at the west end of the south arcade, which consequently has only five arches, whereas there are six arches on the north side. The easternmost arches are early 16th century, when the aisles were extended to form chapels. They still leave one bay of the chancel unflanked and here 14th century windows remain on each side, although the east window is late 15th century. The south aisle is not quite as wide as that on the north and is narrower towards the west, and in fact the outer wall here is partly 14th century, with two windows and a blocked doorway of that date. Three members of the Brock family held the incumbency from 1803 until 1918 and are commemorated by an oak eagle lectern. The oil lamps in the east corners of the chancel are all that remain of a series of 57 lamps before electricity was installed in 1927. There is a tablet in the north aisle to James Perchard, a Gentleman of the Privy Council of Queen Anne and George I, who gave £1000 for "Fonds aux Pauvres de la Paroisse" (poor funds).

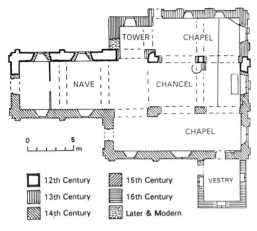

12th Century   15th Century   VESTRY

13th Century   16th Century

14th Century   Later & Modern

Plan of St Sampson's Church

St Saviour's Church

ST SAMPSON

The nave and chancel are mostly 14th century, although 12th century masonry is thought to remain on the north side of each of them. A north transeptal tower of the early 13th century with a saddleback roof opens off the east bay of the nave, which is flanked on the south side by the west bay of a south chapel of the mid 14th century which has a damaged piscina with a six-pointed stair upon one of the voussoirs. The north chapel is late 13th century. Projecting south from the south chapel east bay is an early 16th century two storey vestry with modern windows.

St Sampson's Church

St Saviour's Church

ST SAVIOUR

The nave and chancel with their pilaster buttresses are late 12th century, although the nave west wall is an extension of the mid 15th century. The 13th century south chapel was originally a transept adjoining a former central tower. Of the late 14th century are the small south porch and most of the north aisle with a blocked doorway and one original window, but the aisle east window is slightly later and the western part of the aisle, together with the two western octagonal piers of the arcade and the NW tower are late 15th century. The tower stands over a font brought over from St Peter Port in 1886 and has a rib-vault, an embattled parapet around the base of a lead-covered spire, and a NE turret containing a stair reached through an ogival-headed doorway. A similar doorway (renewed) leaded into the early 16th century vestry projecting north beyond the aisle east bay. The chancel south windows and the five easternmost arches of the arcade (with circular piers, smaller than those further west) are also early 16th century. One mid 13th century window remains east of the porch and the vaults of nave and chancel are probably of that period. There is a 17th century alms box. The stained glass is mostly 20th century.

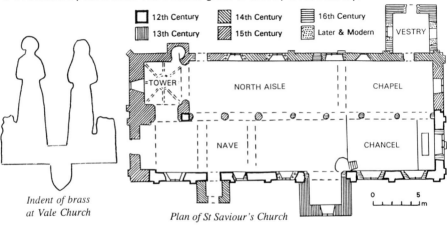

Indent of brass at Vale Church

Plan of St Saviour's Church

TORTEVAL - St Philip

The existing embattled building of grey granite with an east apse and a circular west tower was erected in 1816 to a design by John Wilson, although the weathervane upon the circular spire is older, being dated 1774, and one of the three bells dates from 1432. The small medieval church dedicated to St Mary had a late 12th century nave and chancel with the windows later altered into plain rectangles and a porch added on the south, whilst on the north side was a 13th century aisle ending at the west with a rectangular tower (longest from north to south) with an octagonal spire with corner spirelets.

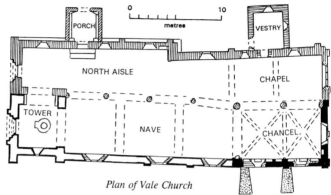

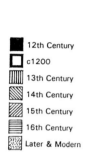

- ■ 12th Century
- □ c1200
- ▥ 13th Century
- ▧ 14th Century
- ▨ 15th Century
- ▤ 16th Century
- ▦ Later & Modern

Plan of Vale Church

Torteval Church

Vale Church

West doorways at Vale Church

VALE - St Michael

The oldest part is the mid 12th century chancel containing re-used Roman bricks., It is rib vaulted in two bays and has seven blind arches (possibly sedilia) on the south side. Settlement has caused some depression of the head of the chancel arch and two large buttresses have been provided on the south side. Originally there was a central pilaster on the east wall with a round-headed window on either side of it, traces of which remain. The nave and west tower were added in the late 12th century. The tower west doorway is round arched and of three plain orders. In the 13th century the nave was given a vault divided into three bays, and a north chapel was added, flanking the chancel and east bay of the nave. Finally, towards the end of that century, an aisle was extended west from the chapel to extend alongside the other two bays of the nave and the tower. The aisle has a west doorway similar to that of the tower, plus a north doorway in front of which a porch was added in the late 15th century. The vestry on the north side of the chapel is early 16th century and there are late 16th century windows in the nave south wall. The eastern two bays of the arcade are early 15th century, the other four bays being late 15th century. The piers of this part have west-facing brackets below the capitals, the most westerly bracket being carved with a lion's head. A dog's head appears on the arch over the pulpit. Just west of the north chapel screen is a floor slab with indents of brasses of a man and his wife with a shield. There are several stained glass windows.

This church seems to have served a priory which was dependency of the Benedictine abbey of Mont St Michel. In 1406 Sir John de Lisle asked the Privy Council for permission to removed timber from a ruined part of the priory buildings for repairs at Castle Cornet. The Crown took the priory away from Mont St Michel in 1413 but continued to appoint priors until at least 1478. A portion of 12th century walling remains near the chancel of the church and the lower part of the end of a 14th century range later converted into cottages remains further to the south.

OTHER OLD CHAPELS & CHURCHES OF GUERNSEY

CHAPELLE DE LORETTE (Parish of St Peter Port)

The house called Lorette near Victoria Tower lies close to the site of a late medieval chapel named in commemoration of a pilgrimage to Loretto in Italy.

CHAPELLE DOM HUE (Parish of St Pierre du Bois)

On a tiny tidal island west of Perelle Bay are footings of a crudely built hermit's cell or chapel. The structure seems to have had stone benches along the longer sides.

LIHOU PRIORY (Parish of St Piere du Bois)

This priory dedicated to St Mary is mentioned in a bull of Adrain IV, the only English Pope, dated 1155, when it belonged to the abbey of Mont St Michel. The priors were appointed by the monastery of St Michael of the Vale. Ruins of the 12th century priory church and a pair of 13th and 14th century domestic buildings to the west of it lie on the south side of an island reached by a tidal causeway on the west side of Guernsey. The church was paved with alternate glazed tiles of green and buff malachite and was used by the inhabitants of Rocquaine and Perelle as a chapel-of-ease when the tides allowed. The nave was rebuilt in the mid 13th century and was then provided with a vault, the last traces of which collapsed in 1979, and a small tower on the north side with two buttresses projecting into the nave. During Queen Elizabeth I's reign a house was erected within the chancel.

NOTRE DAME DE PULAYES (Parish of St Sampson)

Nothing remains of a chapel on the shore north of Noirmont mentioned c1405.

Lihou Priory Church

St Apolline's Chapel

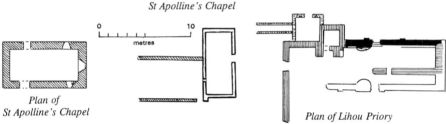

Plan of
St Apolline's Chapel

Plan of Lihou Priory

PLEINHEAME CHAPEL   (Detached part of Vale Parish)

The site of this chapel-of-ease lies in the garden of the house called Le Hamel.

ST APOLLINE'S CHAPEL   (Parish of St Saviour)

This is the only building in the British Isles which is dedicated to Apolline, patron saint of dentists. It is a small rectangular vaulted building with a belfry on the west gable, a piscina in the SE corner, round-headed doorways in the western part of each side wall, and single small rectangular windows facing east, north and south. The chapel probably dates from the 1390s, Nicholas Henry having obtained permission to found it from the Abbey of Mont St Michel (as lord of the manor) in 1392, and from King Richard II in 1394. The south side has faded wall-paintings.

ST BRIOC'S CHAPEL   (Parish of Torteval)

An 18th century gable wall of the late 16th century farmhouse beside the valley leading from Torteval Church to the sea incorporates walling likely to represent the 13th century east wall of the chapel.

ST CLAIR'S CHAPEL   (Parish of Vale)

Beside the Route Militaire is a ruined cottage converted from the much altered east end of a medieval chapel. A semi-circular head from a tiny 12th century window has been found on this site, together with an interesting lintel from the fireplace of the adjoining priest's house.

ST GEORGE'S CHAPEL (Parish of Castel)

Fragments of the east and west walls remain of a 14th century chapel used as a schoolhouse from 1675 until it was demolished in 1790. Mont St Michel had a chapel here beside a holy well in 1156.

ST GERMAIN'S CHAPEL (Parish of Castel)

Nothing remains of a chapel beside a holy well 0.7km north of St George.

ST JACQUES' CHAPEL (Parish of St Peter Port)

The house called Ravenscourt lies on the site. Footings remained in the 19th century.

ST JEAN'S CHAPEL (Parish of St Martin)

The primary school lies on the site of a chapel upon or beside a burial mound.

ST MAGLOIRE'S CHAPEL (Parish of Vale)

Mont St Michel had a chapel here in 1156. St Magloire is said to have been given a third of Guernsey in the sixth century to set up a monastery in honour of St Sampson. The 16th century house called St Magloire (now a store) is thought to have been the priest's house, and stood close to where the chapel lay.

ST PETER PORT - FRANCISCAN FRIARY

Of the friary founded by Richard II there remains only a portion of buttressed walling incorporated into a 19th century bank lie beside Hospital Lane, which was formerly called La Rue des Freres. The fragment could have been the north wall of the church. Other late 16th and 17th century buildings in this vicinity may incorporate parts of the friary domestic buildings. After being dissolved the convent became Elizabeth College, the nave serving as a schoolroom and the chancel as the master's house. The cemetery still survives, although there are no ancient tombs there.

LEPER HOSPITALS

Nothing remains of the hospitals or their chapels beside the shore at the Rue de la Maladerie in St Sampson's parish and on the corner of La Marette Rd in St Saviour's parish, its cemetery being near Fort Richmond.

MANORIAL CHAPELS

The Elizabethan house at Anneville Manor is set at right-angles to the late 13th century house, the west part of which formed the chapel of St Thomas. The doorway of three orders in the east wall of the later house was once the chapel north doorway. Nothing remains in situ of chapels in the houses of St Anne, La Grange, La Haye du Puits, Le Marchant, and Vinchelez de Bas, although most of them have left some relic on or near their sites.

CASTLES OF JERSEY

ELIZABETH CASTLE

Perched on a rock east of the castle is a hermitage where St Helier is said to have lived for fifteen years until he was beheaded by pirates in 555. The existing hermitage chapel probably dates from the 1150s when William Fitz-Hamon founded an abbey where the castle now lies. In 1175 Henry II and the Archbishop of Rouen agreed to reduce the abbey to the rank of a priory dependent upon that of Cherbourg. It does not appear that the site was in any way fortified prior to 1551 when a bulwark or platform for a few guns commanding the harbour was built on top of the boss of rock south of the priory, which was then in a decayed state. In the 1590s the upper ward to the south and east of this bulwark (known as The Mount) was laid out to a design by Paul Ivy. Sir Walter Raleigh, appointed Governor of Jersey in 1600, had the highest praise for Ivy as an engineer. Raleigh named the fort "Isabella Bellissima" in honour of Queen Elizabeth. Within the new fort were erected houses for the use of the Governor of Jersey and the captain of the castle, who bore the title of Lieutenant Governor, and, unlike the Governor, was normally in residence. In 1600-3 the area outside the gate was enclosed to form a barbican with its own outer gateway, known as the Iron Gate. A survey of 1617 lists twenty-two cannon upon the walls. The garrison at that time was equipped with forty-three muskets, twenty bandoliers, forty pikes, thirty-six halberds and forty-eight pole-axes, whilst the magazine contained forty-one barrels of gunpowder.

Elizabeth Castle, looking from the Lower Ward up to the Upper Ward

The west side of the Lower ward of Elizabeth Castle

Between 1626 and 1636 the area around the priory was enclosed to form the lower ward. In the 1640s Governor Sir George Carteret built a chapel within the ruins of the priory church and a detached bulwark was erected at the far north end of the site to defend the causeway across the beach. This bulwark was named Fort Charles in honour of Prince Charles, who lived in the castle during the summer of 1646 after Parliament was victorious over his father Charles I, at least in England. Despite this Sir George continued to hold Jersey for the Royalist cause until a large Parliamentary fleet under Admiral Blake arrived in 1651. It was assumed that a long siege would be required to enforce the submission of Elizabeth Castle but after a short bombardment Sir George was forced to submit when a mortar bomb fired from the foot of the Mont de la Ville broke through the vault of the crypt of the priory church, detonating the gunpowder stored there. The explosion totally demolished all that remained of the priory buildings and robbed the garrison of most of their provisions.

In 1668 the size of the fortress was almost doubled when the long narrow area of land between the outer gate of the lower ward and Fort Charles was enclosed to create the outer ward. A new gunpowder store was erected in the Lower Ward in 1682. In the 1730s the defences were improved by John Henry Bastide and more modern guns supplied. A few years later new barracks, officers quarters, canteen and storehouse were built around a parade square in the lower ward. In 1781 a French force landed at La Rocque and occupied St Helier, capturing the Governor, Moise Corbet. The French compelled Corbet to send documents ordering the castle to surrender but Captain Mulcaster refused to do so, informing the French officer delivering them under a flag of truce that he could not understand French. In the meantime the French were defeated in a battle in the Royal Square, although the officer leading the British troops, Major Peirson, was killed in the engagement. This affair emphasised that Elizabeth Castle could only defend St Helier against an attack by sea, rather than overland from elsewhere in Jersey. The result was that Fort Regent was erected on the Mont de la Ville between 1806 and 1814. Elizabeth Castle thus lost its importance. It was however used by the Germans in 1940-45 as a punishment camp and some new gun-positions were created in 1942-4 using Russian slave labour, and a fire control tower set upon the Mount. The castle is now an ancient monument administered by the States of Jersey Public Services Committee.

The upper ward, Elizabeth Castle   *The Governor's House, Elizabeth Castle*

The Outer Ward from the North-East

Plan of Elizabeth Castle

The NE side of the Lower Ward

The entrance to the Upper Ward at Elizabeth Castle   *Sentry Box, Outer Ward*

The castle is reached by a causeway 1km long which is dry for about five hours at a time but at high tide is covered by up to 4m of water. There is a ferry service for visitors using amphibious vehicles. The Outer Gate dating from 1668 is surmounted by a bell of 1797 and flanked by the NE Bastion on one side and the formerly independent Fort Charles on the other. The Guard House inside dates from c1810, as does the Hospital lying further south in the middle of the 210m long Outer Ward with the East Bastion behind it. An intermediate wall across the outer ward connects the Hospital to the West Bastion opposite and is pierced by King William's Gate of 1697, which was widened by the Germans in 1942. Boldly corbelled out from the outermost corner of the NE Bastion is an 18th century brick sentry-box with a domed roof. This bastion was altered by the Germans to take a searchlight, which when not required was wheeled down a railway track to a bomb-proof shelter just north of the hospital. The West Bastion is fitted with musket loops and a urinal. Further south is another bastion with a corner sentry box, within is a bunker of the 1940s armed with a 10.5cm gun. The Outer Ward here attains its greatest width of 80m. There is a third sentry box on the outer corner of the Mount Bastion beside the entrance to the Lower Ward. In the outer ward between these two places is the Grand Battery, created in 1770 to mount very heavy cannon, now represented by replica carronades.

The Lower Ward houses the principal buildings of the castle and is entered by a gateway beside the Mount Bastion at the NE corner. The gate had a drawbridge of the 1730s which withdrew on rollers under the gates. On the north side of the ward is a fine barrack block of 1749, and on the south side are the Officers Quarters, behind which is the Green Bastion, the site of a German searchlight, and having a postern reached by steps on its west flank. A casemate for a 10.5cm gun backs onto the Royal Bastion at the SE corner, the southern part of the parapet of which was cut down to clear a fire of fire for the gun. The cross in the middle of the Lower Ward is the only reminder of the former priory which stood here. Drawings made by Hollar just a year before the explosion which cleared the site in 1651 show that the priory church had lean-to side aisles and a clerestory above, the only instance of such a layout in the Channel Islands. West of the cross is a well-head, but the water from this supply was of poor quality and in the early 19th century the Board or Ordnance supplemented the supply by building tanks to collect rainwater.

Steps up from the Iron Gate at the SW corner of the Lower Ward lead up to a platform in front of Queen Elizabeth's Gate, which is the entrance to the Upper Ward, set in a re-entrant angle allowing it to be flanked. The gate is round arched and was closed by a portcullis. The arms of Sir Anthony Paulet, Governor of Jersey from 1590 until replaced by Sir Walter Raleigh in 1600 appear on one side and above a hoodmould with a fleur-de-lys, above which is a panel with the Royal Arms with the Tudor Rose above it. Steps up from the gate rise to a small court with the Captain's House almost opposite on the north side and the Governor's House to the east. Both date from c1600 and nestle against the rock on which lies the Mount, originally a position for four cannon. The date 1601 is scratched onto the rock beside the steps up to the Mount. Upon it is a Gunnery Control Tower built by the Germans. The Upper Ward appeared larger until the western bastions were filled in and given mountings for a pair of 19th century 7" muzzle loading guns superseded by anti-aircraft guns in the 1940s. In the 1870s a breakwater 600m long was extended out south from below the Upper Ward beyond the rock on which lies the Hermitage.

The east side of the Lower Ward of Elizabeth Castle

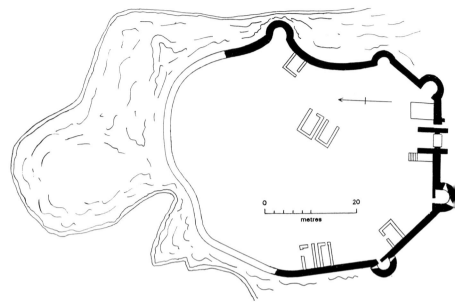

Plan of Grosnez Castle

Grosnez Castle

Grosnez Castle

GROSNEZ CASTLE

This stronghold lies on a promontory at the NW tip of Jersey and is thought to have been built in the early 14th century to serve this part of the island as a refuge. Around an irregularly shaped court about 50m across are remains of a curtain wall 1.7m thick, although little remains of it on the north and west sides. There and also on the east the ground descends precipitously for about 60m straight into the sea. On the south side are the partly reconstructed ruins of a gatehouse about 6.5m wide projecting within the court. There is a portcullis groove descending to passage level, and below the groove is a pit for a counterpoise type drawbridge. Usually such a pit would be placed in front of a portcullis, since if it were possible for an attacker to get underneath the portcullis it would not be much use as a barrier. Each end of the short section of wall which has the gatehouse in the middle ends in a D-shaped tower now reduced to about 2m high. Only that to the west properly flanks the wall, and it has remains of two shooting slits at ground level. Between the gatehouse and the east tower is a ramp up to the former wall-walk. There are two other towers further round on the east and west sides, but beyond them the natural defences made flanking towers superfluous. The castle may not have been permanently occupied and the only traces of internal buildings are of modest structures, so there may never have been a hall or chapel. The spring nearby outside the wall was probably the only water supply apart from what could be retained in cisterns. The castle is said to have been captured by a French force led by the Duke of Bourbon in July 1373 in conjunction with an attack on Mont Orgueil by Bertrand du Guesclin. The building is assumed to have been a ruin since at least the 16th century.

Grosnez Castle

Grosnez Castle

LES CATEAUX

The farm of Les Cateaux lies by a road junction 1km east of Trinity Church. To the NE across the road from the farm is an overgrown earthwork of uncertain date and purpose, although it looks like a ringwork about 30m across on top, the southern half of which has been destroyed. This earthwork lies just west of the centre of an outer enclosure about 500m across defined by a rampart and ditch, although on the south and west sides little of it survives. Here in 1406 the men of Jersey met an combined invading force of Frenchmen under Hector de Pontbriand and Spaniards under Pero Nino and agreed to pay them a ransom for the safety of their lands and possessions.

MONT ORGUEIL CASTLE

This fortress is first mentioned in 1212 when King John appointed Philip d'Aubigny as Warden of the Isles. It is alternatively known as Gorey Castle. It is likely that King John began construction work here soon after losing Normandy in 1204. The castle is next mentioned in 1232 when Philip d'Aubigny was re-appointed for another term as Warden and took over command of the castle from Gerard de Lambersard. In 1294, following an attack on Jersey by the French Admirals Jean d'Harcourt and Mathieu de Montmorency, the castle was repaired and new walls were constructed by the outer gate. In 1323 the elderly Warden Otto de Grandison was ordered by Edward II to go to Mont Orgueil to investigate complaints by the islanders against his unpopular lieutenants. After John de Roches was appointed Warden in 1327 he carried out some work around the NE postern. In 1331 he was accused of spending too much on the works at the castle but was exonerated. The French invaded Jersey in 1338 and 1339, but the castle, commanded by Renaud de Carteret, held out.

The Middle Ward at Mont Orgueil Castle

The Middle Ward Gatehouse from the Keep

In 1373 William de Asthorp and a small garrison of twenty men-at-arms and few archers resisted an attack by a French force led by Bertram du Guesclin. The outer ward was stormed after the wall was breached but the defenders held still held out and agreed to terms upon which they would have surrendered if the English fleet had not arrived within two months. When the King's Receiver, Thomas de Appleby finally arrived to pay the garrison in 1375 one of them stabbed him in the neck. The French made another attack on Jersey in 1406 together with a party of Spaniards. They decided not to attack the castle but took a ransom from the islanders. After Edward, Duke of York, deposed his Lancastrian rival Henry VI and took his throne in 1461, the Lancastrian Warden of the Isles, John Nanfan, handed over the castle to the French, although the full circumstances remain obscure. In 1462 there is a mention of cannon at the castle and in 1463 Jean de Carbonnel, lieutenant of the Grand Seneschal of Normandy, Pierre de Maulevrier, held a court in the castle to investigate an alleged plot to restore Jersey to the English. The English Crown only regained the castle in 1468 after a five month blockade by a fleet under Vice-Admiral Richard Harliston working in conjunction with a force of islanders led by Philip de Carteret. The office of Warden of the Isles was abolished in 1470 and the bailiwicks of Guernsey and Jersey were given separate Governors, Richard Harliston being appointed to command Jersey. The tower named after him was built around this time. After Richard III's death and death in 1485 Harliston refused to hand over the castle to Henry VII's commissioner Edward Weston, and his garrison had to be starved until submission.

In 1515 the islanders complained about the considerable levies needed to repair the castle, which is said to have been neglected during the period 1497-1500 when Thomas Overay was Governor. A commission sent by Henry VIII in 1531 reported that both the castle and its garrison were in an unsatisfactory state. Governor Sir Hugh Vaughan was recalled in 1532, but his replacement Sir Anthony Ughtred died shortly afterwards. Edward Seymour, Duke of Somerset was later made Governor and under his lieutenant Henry Cornish work began on updating the defences. In 1551 six soldiers of the garrison fled to Normandy after a state of robberies in Jersey, including a raid on the house of the Bailiff, Helier de Carteret, but they were soon returned to Jersey and hanged. The great rampart replacing the original north and west walls of the inner ward is probably the work commenced after a report was drawn up for Queen Elizabeth in 1562. By 1567 almost £4,000 had been spent on remodelling the castle. In 1573 Sir Amyas Paulet, who had succeeded his father Hugh as Governor two years earlier, reported that the new works were only two thirds complete and asked for another £400 for work to be executed that year, and the same for the following year. In 1594 the Privy Council decided that money spent on defences for Jersey would be better used on developing Elizabeth Castle, since Mont Orgueil was vulnerable to a bombardment from the nearby higher ground. The governor was ordered to transfer his residence to Elizabeth Castle as soon as his house there was completed. However, this new residence was not completed until about the time when Sir Walter Raleigh was appointed Governor in 1600. He took a liking to Mont Orgueil and recommended it to be retained instead of dismantled, calling it "a stately fort of great capacatye" and commenting that "it were a pitty to cast it down having cost Her Majestie's father, brother and sister with her own charge 20,000 marks the erectinge". In 1611, under Governor Sir John Peyton (who succeeded Raleigh in 1603), there was a garrison of 34 men. It was reduced to 19 in 1617, and on one visit during that year Bailiff John Herault found just four men in the castle. He recommended to the Privy Council rates of pay of £500 a year for the castle Captain, £60 for the Minister, £30 for the Master Porter, £15 for the Master Gunner, and two and a half pence per day for each of 40 soldiers. Some repairs were executed and the West Bulwark begun in the 1590s finally completed. William Prynne was imprisoned in the castle from 1638 to 1640 for his opposition to Charles I.

Crypt at Mont Orgueil Castle

Mont Orgueil Castle

At the start of the Civil War Sir Philip de Carteret fortified Elizabeth Castle for King Charles whilst his wife commanded Mont Orgueil. Parliament sent over Major Lydcott who began setting up siegeworks for a bombardment of Mont Orgueil. The garrison sallied and captured the works, and the major only just managed to escape. Support for the Parliamentary cause on Jersey subsequently waned and the castle was left in peace. In 1645 the Parliamentarian Dean of Jersey, David Bandinel, and his son James, Rector of St Mary, attempted to escape from imprisonment in Prynne's Tower but fell onto the rocks below since the rope they had made by knotting their bed-clothes together proved too short. The castle was found to be unfit to accommodate Prince Charles during his stay on Jersey during the summer of 1646. Charles visited Mont Orgueil, and was there again in 1649 after being proclaimed king upon the execution of his father. In 1651 Admiral Blake brought Colonel Heane over to Jersey with 3,000 men to take control of the island for Parliament. Colonel Philip Carteret was offered generous terms to surrender the castle, and, since his garrison was unreliable, he accepted them. The castle was subsequently used as a prison. Colonel John Lilburne was sent to it in 1654, and George Villiers, 2nd Duke of Buckingham was kept at Mont Orgueil before being transferred to the Tower of London. Charles II later incarcerated several signatories to his father's execution in the castle. The Bailiff and Jurats later complained to King Charles that the garrison under Sir John Lanier in Mont Orgueil was given to "drinking to excesse" and that all kinds of immorality and impropriety was taking place. Jurat Philip Dumaresq's "Survey of ye Island of Jersey" for James II in 1685 described the castle guns as having perished carriages and that the place was only suitable to be a barracks for a company of foot. However in 1691 it was reported that the castle was so dilapidated that it was not possible to accommodate troops, and it ceased around then to function as a prison.

Repairs were finally executed in 1730-4 under the engineer John Henry Bastide. During the Napoleonic Wars Admiral Philip d'Auvergne ran a secret service in Brittany and Normandy from his headquarters in Mont Orgueil. In 1794 the castle guns fired upon a French frigate which was escorting a convoy from St Malo to Cherbourg. In 1801 the King Charles Battery collapsed onto the beach, necessitating some rebuilding. By the 1830s visitors were paying admission fees which were put towards repairs. In 1846 the visitors included Queen Victoria and Prince Albert. The Crown transferred the building to the States of Jersey for preservation as an ancient monument in 1907, but it was used as an Observation Post during World War I. After their invasion in 1940 the Germans initially just placed a look-out on the top of the keep but in 1942 the castle was made into a strongpoint with barrack-rooms in the keep, upon which was built a fire control tower.

As built in the early 13th century the castle comprised an inner ward (now known as the Middle Ward) on the highest part of the precipitous rock overlooking Gorey Harbour on the east side of Jersey, and a lower ward to the SW. This in turn was reached through outer ward with a gateway facing north, in front of which was a rock-cut ditch up to 3m deep. It is likely that the outer ward originally had a palisade and it may not have been fully enclosed by stone walls until the 1330s. This part was subsequently much rebuilt and the existing 16th century line of defence encloses a smaller area than the earlier wall, which once enclosed the well now lying outside. The bank upon which the curtain original lay was cut back when houses were built against it in the 1820s. The gateway is commanded by the U-shaped Harliston Tower built c1470 and intended to be armed with cannon. In front are footings of a 16th century outwork which protected the outer drawbridge. A long open passage then leads to the original outer gateway, the Harliston Tower having been built out in front of it. Beside this gate are remains of the Picardy Half-Moon Bastion.

The outer ward had a south wall about 70m long flanked at each end by a round tower about 6m in diameter. The central part of this wall, known as the King Charles' Battery, collapsed onto the beach in 1802 and a new wall was built further north, reducing the size of the ward. The NW wall of the ward is bowed in at the centre, where there is a square gatehouse, and meets what remains of the south wall at an acute angle covered by a tower, below which lies the Water Battery built in 1802 on the site of an older outwork. The gateway was closed by a counterpoise type drawbridge and a portcullis. According to a report of 1611 the Lower Ward once contained twenty houses in which prominent citizens of Jersey could take refuge in times of war, but at present the only building here is the Porter's Lodge west of the gateway, now used as the shop.

Mont Orgueil Castle

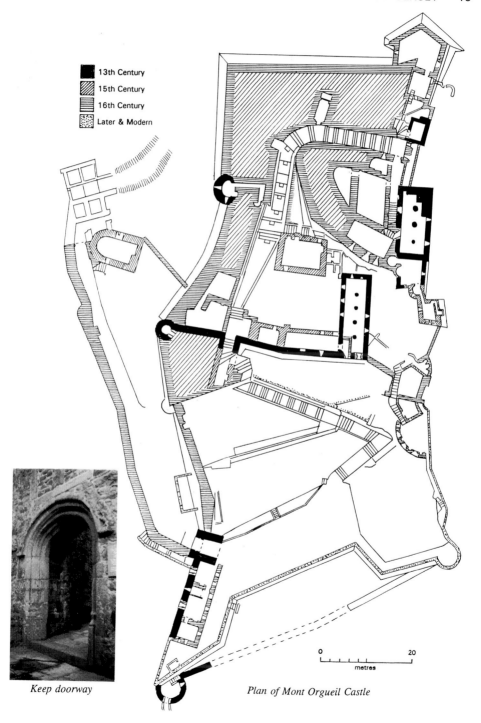

13th Century
15th Century
16th Century
Later & Modern

Keep doorway

Plan of Mont Orgueil Castle

0   20
metres

The wall between the Lower and Middle Wards is about 60m long and had a round tower at the NW end, whilst at the SE end lay the Busgros Tower, a composite rectangular structure awkwardly grafted onto the rock and containing one large upper room with a flat roof surrounded by a wall-walk and parapet. Steps down from the Busgros Tower lead to the Cornish Bastion which extends halfway down the east side of the Lower Ward and bears the date 1547 and the arms of Henry Cornish, Lieutenant Governor from 1541 to 1549. The gatehouse lies close to the round tower and was originally a rectangular tower with the passage closed as its inner end by a portcullis and the outer arch flanked by pilaster buttresses, it being approached directly by a flight of steps up the rock. A number of rooms were built against the curtain wall inside, two of which were guard rooms flanking a wider and probably open extension of the passage. In the 15th century the gatehouse was lengthened on the outside and given an outer doorway closed by a portcullis in its NW side. The outer end of the building was then given a machicolated parapet. In the 16th century this new outer entrance was blocked and an approach was ramped up from beside the Cornish Bastion to a doorway pierced through on the SE side of the gatehouse extension. This doorway has above it the arms of Queen Elizabeth with the date 1593. The north corner of the Lower Ward, i.e. the space west of the gateway was later closed off to form Peyton's Bulwark, upon which cannon were mounted.

In its original form the Middle Ward was about 70m long and mostly about 45m wide. A lofty late 16th century rampart of earth enclosed by stone walls now fills up the NE and NW sides. The original NE curtain bowed out in the middle to a tower and there were probably towers at each end, whilst the NW side bowed inwards. The central tower here still survives against the outer face of the later rampart, and now has a bell on top of it. There are traces of a medieval outwork which helped protect the north corner, which was exposed to attack, despite being perched on a rock face. The wide rampart and the mid 16th century keep, with just a ramp leading up between them, take up most of the former open space of the Middle Ward, which has been reduced to a small court behind the wall dividing two wards. Amongst the buildings here is a vaulted undercroft, above which was the chapel of St George, of which little remains, and a building of uncertain purpose, but referred to as St George's Hall. A well 17m deep is reached from the ramp leading up to the keep. At the top of the ramp there is access to a postern down onto an outwork built in the 1330s (but remodelled later) below the east corner, which in the late 16th century was given a bastion to flank the main rampart. A headquarters building erected by the Germans over the postern and bastion has been removed.

At the top of the rampart is a doorway into the complex of apartments known as the keep set on the highest point of the rock. This doorway has a portcullis groove and is surmounted by a plaque with the date 1551. The doorway leads through to a narrow passage between the two parts of the building. The original 13th century part lies on the SE, facing an almost sheer drop into the sea. It consists of a hall built over a vaulted undercroft with a line of central piers, reached through a porch on the NW side, and having a suite of two chambers beyond to the SW in a block with a corbelled parapet, on the other side of which was another wing (Prynne's Tower) containing chambers, these latter parts only being joined by the spiral staircase in a turret called the Watch Tower between them. At the other end of the hall a passage led out to two more chambers in the NE tower. This tower was converted into a magazine in 1717 and its openings and the access to it from the hall were then blocked. The hall was itself later provided with a vault. It is sometimes described as being the chapel of St Mary, and may have been used as such at one time, although this can hardly have been its original function. This room was fitted up a barrack for sixty men in 1778.

Part of keep at Mont Orgueil   *Domestic buildings at Mont Orgueil*

    With improvements in the power of cannon during the late 15th and early 16th centuries the domestic apartments became vulnerable to bombardment from Mont St Nicholas not far to the NW. To protect the rooms a massive D-shaped block about 20m wide was built in front but before long this in turn was deemed to need shielding, hence the massive and lofty rampart just across the approach ramp, although the rampart never carried enough guns to seriously threaten an enemy setting up a battery on Mont St Nicholas. The round cornered outer part of the new keep (the Somerset Tower) is solid for up to 7m, behind which are rooms. Those adjoining the central passage have been roofless since at least the mid 18th century, creating a court onto which windows from roofless rooms further NW now open, but the four storeys of chambers on the SW side remain intact, with numerous two-light square-headed windows with typically Tudor-type hoodmoulds facing the Middle Ward. The topmost room was reserved for the Captain or Governor. It has two typically Tudor fireplaces and was probably originally divided into two rooms.

Royal Arms, Mont Orgueil

ST AUBIN'S FORT

A U-shaped blockhouse with the round end facing SW was erected on a reef on the west side of St Aubin's Bay in 1542. There is access via a causeway at low tide. The blockhouse is about 13m long by 12m wide and now lies against the NW side of a fort about 50m long by 30m wide built around it by the Royalists after they captured the place in a surprise attack in 1643. They held the fort until it was surrendered without a fight to a Parliamentary fleet under Admiral Blake in 1651. The blockhouse was converted by the Royalists into a tower with a new gun position on top, the old gunports being blocked and the space from which they were operated being converted into a store. A new entrance was made on the SE side, towards the courtyard, since the fort NW wall blocked the original entrance. This later entrance now lacks its ladder and access is now through a former SW facing gunport. The gateway to the fort, dating in its present form from 1742, lies at the east end of the SE side, inside of which was formerly a wooden barrack block. This is the side least well flanked although covering fire was originally possible from the easternmost of three bastions group together at the south end. The Germans mounted a searchlight on this bastion (which has a latrine block adjoining it) and set up a tank turret gun west of it. Another wooden barrack block with a store and cistern underneath lay between the tower and the South-West Bastion. The fort was re-armed in 1838, and traversing guns were set up on the North-East Bastion, on the North-West Bastion and on each of the three southern bastions, whilst the polygonal north bastion covering the wharves built in the 18th century was pierced for musketry. The fort is used as an activity centre for young people and the interior is not open to the public.

St Aubin's Fort

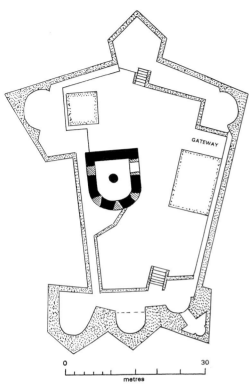

Entrance to St Aubin's Fort

Plan of St Aubin's Fort

ST OUEN'S MANOR

The Carteret family had a house on Jersey by 1135, presumably on the present site. The house was allowed to decay during the French occupation of Jersey in the 1461 and in 1483 was rebuilt by Philippe de Carteret. He gained royal permission for crenellation on the grounds that the house was vulnerable to French raids, being very close to the sea. The thinly walled central block perhaps of this period is flanked by two equally thinly walled towers, one of which contains a staircase. It is not really a defensible building, although the garden to the SW has a high retaining wall of defensive aspect to the south and west and the provision of a ditch on the other sides of the house might have been sufficient for security against minor raids. The former yard to the north with pens for animals seems to have been of medieval origin. Much of the rest is 17th century, the wings flanking the entrance being of 1670. The Carterets have provided Jersey over the years with fifteen Bailiffs, several Lieutenant-Governors and 48 Jurats, the majority of them christened either Philippe or Renaud. A datestone of 1661 has initials of Sir Philippe, knighted by Prince Charles in 1646. The oldest building at the manor is the early 14th century chapel of St Anne. It was restored in the 19th century but the east window and two doorways on the north side are original. There is no vaulting. The altar slab has come from the vanished chapel of St George at Vinchelez de Bas Manor, first mentioned in 1156.

OLD CHURCHES OF JERSEY

GROUVILLE - St Martin

The nave, crossing, and chancel are all mid 12th century. The nave has no vault, being covered by a wooden roof of 1840-3. There are two original north windows and others can be traced opposite them on the south side. The south windows are modern but there is an early 16th century window on the north side. The tower and spire were cement rendered in 1788, the tower spire having long narrow lucarnes, whilst the tower contains a clock with east and west faces. In the 15th century a west porch was added, then a north chapel, and finally a new east end was built with a four-light window, whilst a three-light window with reticulated tracery was inserted into the east wall of the late 14th century south chapel. There are gargoyles on the outside of the chancel. The arch between the chancel and south chapel is early 16th century. The chapel contains a recess with a head with a hole in the forehead and has traces of wall-paintings. The unusual font with a subsidiary basin within the main one was transferred here from La Hougue Bie after that site was purchased by La Societe Jersiaise, but it probably originally came from the church at St Helier. The granite bowl of the original 14th or 15th century font now forms a memorial under the crossing. The church has much 19th century stained glass. The memorials include those of Sir Herbert Lunsford, Lieutenant-Governor from 1675 until his death in 1680, a tablet to John Williams, d1786, and his wife Mary, d1783, and a tablet to francis Payn, Dean of Jersey, d1775. The churchyard contains a memorial to soldiers of the 83rd Regiment killed by the French at Platte Rocque in 1781.

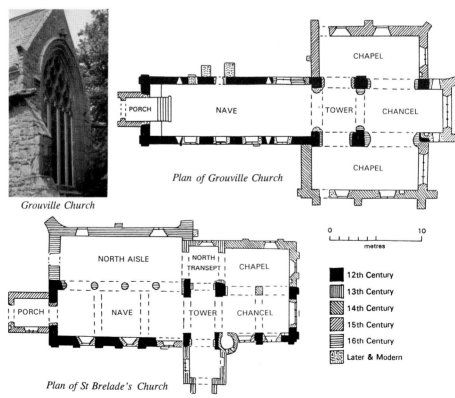

Grouville Church

Plan of Grouville Church

NAVE

PORCH

TOWER

CHANCEL

CHAPEL

CHAPEL

0   10
metres

NORTH AISLE

NORTH TRANSEPT

CHAPEL

PORCH

NAVE

TOWER

CHANCEL

■ 12th Century

▥ 13th Century

▨ 14th Century

▩ 15th Century

▤ 16th Century

▦ Later & Modern

Plan of St Brelade's Church

St Brelade's Church

Grouville Church

ST BRELADE

The nave, crossing and chancel are all of the mid 12th century, but the double piscina in the chancel is late 13th century. The nave has six closely spaced pilaster buttresses on the south side. The rectangular tower has a saddle-back roof, the upper chamber being reached by a stair in a 15th century conical-roofed circular turret at the SE corner. Off this stair led a doorway (now blocked) to a loft over a screen, for which corbels remain on either side of the chancel arch. The transepts are 13th century, that on the south having an altar recess in the east wall. The two bay north chapel, loftier than the chancel, is early 14th century, whilst the wider north aisle with a four bay arcade of pointed arches on circular piers is a replacement of 1537 of a narrower older aisle. The aisle west doorway arch is adorned with a cable-moulding. The porches built against the end walls of the south transept and nave are 15th century, the west porch having a holy water stoup. Until then the nave was entered through a south doorway, traces of which were found in 1895 below the westernmost window on the south side. The octagonal late medieval font was restored to the church after being discovered amongst bushes above the church by a picnic party in 1845. The interior of the church has been stripped of its plaster. There are many stained glass memorial windows. Other memorials include a tomb chest of Jean Baillehache, d1652, in the south transept, and a tablet to Marie Bartlett, whose husband Francis, d1741, found the General Hospital.

St Clement's Church

ST CLEMENT

This is the smallest of the medieval churches on Jersey. The early 12th century nave has one original window on the north side, where a sequence of four pilaster buttresses remains. Two other windows there are early 14th century. A wall painting there depicts St Michael and the Dragon. The central tower is late 12th century but the east and west arches under it were remodelled in the 15th century, when the crossing was given a rib-vault and the 12th century chancel south wall was doubled in thickness by adding to both sides. Also 15th century are the east wall with a three light window and the two bay arcade to the north chapel. On the spandrel over the octagonal pier is the Payn arms. This chapel, now housing the organ and vestry, is early 14th century, although its east window is 15th century. It has an arch broken through the east wall of the 13th century north transept, thus destroying the central part of a wall-painting depicting St Margaret and St Barbara. The south transept of the same period has an altar recess in the east wall, and fragments of another wall painting of the Three Living and the Three Dead on the west wall. The fine late medieval font with traceried panels was discovered buried in the churchyard in the mid 19th century. The monuments include a tablet to Helier Dumaresq, d1716, and his daughter Esther, d1717, and there are several stained glass memorial windows of the late 19th and early 20th century. Against the chancel south wall outside is a tomb chest with the dates 1596 and 1606 and the names of Jean Dumaresq and his wife Ester with shields with the badges of the Payns (trefoils), Dumaresqs (scallop shells), Bagots (dolphins), and the arms of the Payns and Lemprieres.

St Clement's Church

Font at St Clement's

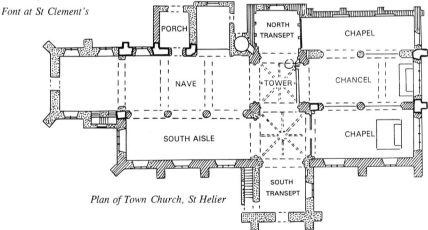

Plan of Town Church, St Helier

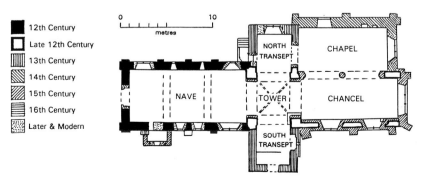

■	12th Century
□	Late 12th Century
	13th Century
	14th Century
	15th Century
	16th Century
	Later & Modern

0   10
metres

Plan of St Clement's Church

Town Church, St Helier

ST HELIER

Known in Jersey as the Town Church, this building was heavily restored in 1864-8, when a new south transept was built beyond the old one and the nave extended westwards by two bays. These extensions are the only parts not vaulted. Some 12th century masonry remains in the chancel east wall and the nave north wall. The north transept with internal arcading on the east and west walls is early 13th century and the north chapel now containing the organ is late 13th century, although its two bay arcade is Victorian. The crossing tower and south aisle with a three bay arcade are mid 15th century and the south chapel with a two bay arcade is late 15th century. The north porch also contains 15th century work. A modern vestry now adjoins it to the east. The tower has a straight parapet with quatrefoil openings. The church has a rich collection of 20th century stained glass windows, 19th and 20th century furnishings. The monuments include those of Maximilian Norreys, who died in 1591 whilst serving in the army of Henry IV of France, a slate to Garthruda Amy, wife of Captain Thomas Amy, d1647, John Durell, d1725 and his wife Elizabeth, d1724, and a monument of c1750 probably by Sir Henry Cheere to Magdalene Durell, widow of Sir Edward de Carteret. Nothing remains of a chapel mentioned in 1548 as standing by the rectory in the churchyard NW corner.

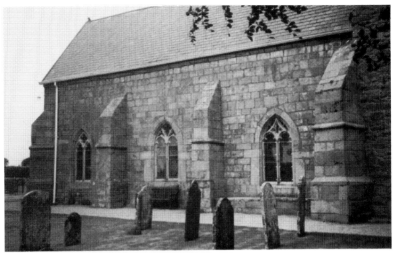

St John's Church

ST JOHN

The mid 16th century north aisle now serves as the nave and the 15th century north chapel with 17th century windows has become the chancel. The original nave was rebuilt in the 17th century. It has an arcade with two pointed arches on circular piers spaced as if for a four bay arcade, but instead there is just a single wide round third arch for the eastern half, apparently the result of an alteration in 1849 to allow a better view of the pulpit. The arches between the old chancel and present one are 15th century. The former chancel is 12th century, like the central tower, and has a vault of the early 16th century. This part was rebuilt outside in 1853 and provided with a small porch. At the NE corner of the present chancel is a blocked doorway (probably for a former vestry) and the date 1622 with initials J.L.B. In the 1970s the rendering was taken off the spire and a parish room was added on the north side. There is a holy water stoup close to the doorway to the parish room. The west side of the spire bears the arms of Thomas Lempriere, Bailiff of Jersey in 1495. The pulpit is of 1791 but was cut down to its present size in 1921. Several windows have 20th century memorial stained glass. Other memorials include those of Josue Le Couteur, d1675, Abraham de Carteret, d1681, Lord of La Hougue Boete, and Clement Lempriere, d1715.

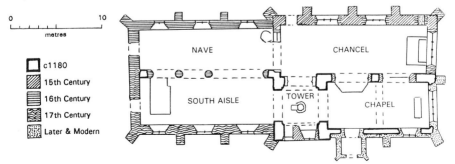

Plan of St John's Church

ST LAWRENCE

The nave and the saddle-back roofed central tower are mid 12th century. The south transept with an altar recess in its east wall and the west portal are 13th century. The inner doorway of the portal was segmental-headed until altered in the 1890s, when the tower top was restored by J.E.Trollope. In the 13th century the nave vault was added, with doubleaux dividing off the end bays. There are traces of a former south doorway of that period. The chancel is late 13th century but has been mostly rebuilt apart from the four-light east window of the late 15th century. In the 1520s, at the expense of Rector Louis Hamptonne, the north transept was rebuilt larger than before and given a NW stair turret and a north chapel built east of it with a two bay arcade to the chancel. The chapel is dated 1524 on the NE buttress and bears the Hamptonne arms on one of the bosses of the rib-vault, whilst another has a Tudor Rose. The north aisle with a four bay arcade towards the nave was added in 1546. These parts have original windows and the aisle has a wide blocked west doorway. Heads in the corners of the chapel probably represent Henry VIII, Catherine of Aragon and Princess Mary, and there is a comic head in the north transept. In 1891 part of an engaged Doric column was found upon which an epitaph was carved c1600 and then later on a decorative design. The column must have been brought over from outside Jersey. There are several commemorative stain glass windows.

West front of St Lawrence's Church

Interior of St Lawrence's Church

West portal at St Lawrence's Church

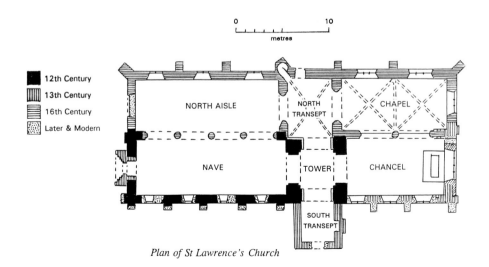

Plan of St Lawrence's Church

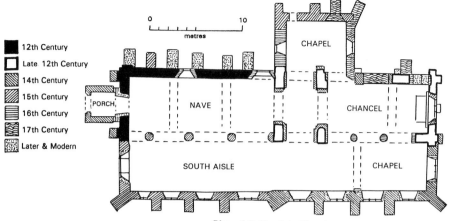

12th Century

Late 12th Century

14th Century

15th Century

16th Century

17th Century

Later & Modern

Plan of St Martin's Church

ST MARTIN

Six heavy buttresses prop up the leaning north wall of the Norman nave. The crossing and chancel are also 12th century, but probably later. The vaults were inserted in the 13th century, when the west doorway was deepened outwards, whilst the east window dates from c1430. In the late 14th century a west porch was added, the crossing arches were remodelled and the south transept swept away by the addition of a south chapel with diagonal corner buttresses. There was at that time a north chapel, shorter than its counterpart. The present north chapel named after Rector Richard Mabon, d1543, is a still shorter rebuild of the 15th, 16th and 17th centuries with heavy buttressing. There is a carved face above the reset 15th century east window of the chapel. Also heavily buttressed is the early 15th century south aisle. It has an arcade of three arches plus a much lower and narrower one at the west end. One of the buttresses has a weathered heraldic monument, and there is a sundial of 1736 nearby. The central tower has an octagonal spire and a clock of 1903.

St Martin's Church

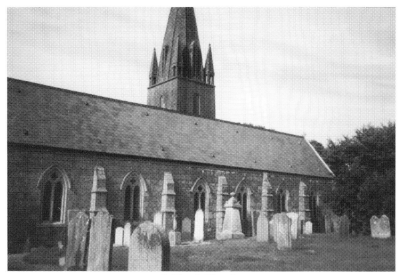

St Mary's Church

ST MARY

The 12th century nave and chancel have now become a north aisle and Lady Chapel. The latter has traces of original east windows either side of the existing east window. A south chapel with a single wide arch to the former chancel and a narrow arch to the crossing tower was added in the 16th century. This chapel had a fourth western bay flanking the east end of the former nave. At its east end is a piscina adorned with rope moulding and an Easter Sepulchre, whilst there is a holy water stoup further west, and on the gable outside is the date 1342 in Roman numerals. In a 19th century remodelling this chapel was extended by two more bays to the west end and became the nave and chancel. Also 19th century are the outer parts of the west doorway, the north windows, and the north porch beside the tower with a staircase on the west and a small vestry to the east. The date 1834 appears on the NE one of a set of four corner pinnacles on round arches at the foot of a hexagonal spire with a weathercock. There are monuments to Rector Daniel Gruchy, d1677, and Rector Thomas La Breton, d1728, whilst outside the west wall is a gravestone with an effigy of a medieval priest with a chalice and fish. On the south wall is a sundial of 1763.

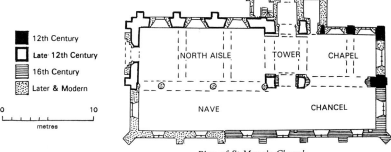

Plan of St Mary's Church

St Ouen's Church

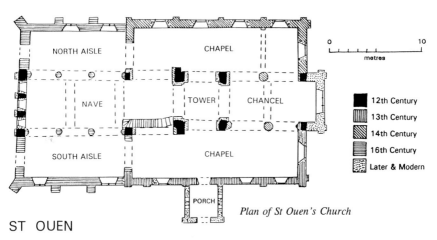

Plan of St Ouen's Church

ST OUEN

The crossing under the tower goes back to the mid 12th century, although the piers have been partly refaced. The nave west wall is also 12th century, but the windows and pilaster buttresses there are modern. There are two gargoyles here and there is a chimney pot on the gable apex instead of a cross. The original transepts were absorbed into the south and north chapels of the late 13th and early 14th centuries respectively. These chapels have two bays of almost round arches towards the chancel, and also flank the eastern part of the nave. The three bay aisles with arcades of pointed arcades on circular piers are mid 16th century and until then the western two thirds of the nave was aisleless. The chancel has a mid 13th century vault and a modern east end. The porch projecting beyond where the south transept once was is also modern but upon it are two old carved heads, one bearded. A feature of the interior is the stone staircase rising within the nave SE corner to give access to the upper parts of the tower. There is a brass inscription to Sir Philip de Carteret, d1643. The north chapel contains a marble top of a tomb chest of Elizabeth Wilson, d1719, the seven-year-old daughter of Robert Wilson, Lieutenant-Governor of Jersey. In the south chapel is a granite stone to Rector Peter de la Place, d1681.

ST PETER

Of the 12th century church there remain the nave west wall with two original windows, the crossing tower carrying a spire 36m high, and the chancel. The west doorway incorporates two old gravestones and another, carved with a cross, hammer, pincers and two horseshoes, is built into the 16th century buttress to the south. The tower has windows and then long slits above. The spire was struck by lightning in 1612, 1843 and 1848. The long transepts and the vaults of the nave and chancel are early 13th century. The late 13th century north chapel (now the sacristy) has two recesses in the north wall inside. The chancel has early 14th century south windows and a 15th century east window. The wide and lofty south aisle with a four bay arcade is early 16th century. Below the three-light window at the east end of the south side is a piscina. A vestry is now partitioned off at the west end of it. In 1886 a new north aisle was provided in place of an older aisle just one bay long. At that time extra space was needed to take the men from the former St Peter's Barracks. The monuments include a floriated cross-slab, a cartouche to Elias de Carteret, d1640, and his wife Elizabeth Dumaresq, d1639, several other Dumaresq tablets and a 17th century monument describing Clement Le Montais as a rich merchant.

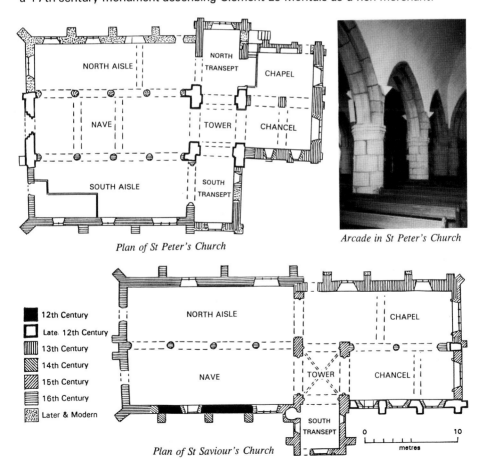

Plan of St Peter's Church

Arcade in St Peter's Church

12th Century
Late 12th Century
13th Century
14th Century
15th Century
16th Century
Later & Modern

NORTH AISLE

NAVE

SOUTH AISLE

NORTH TRANSEPT

CHAPEL

TOWER

CHANCEL

SOUTH TRANSEPT

NORTH AISLE

NAVE

CHAPEL

TOWER

CHANCEL

SOUTH TRANSEPT

Plan of St Saviour's Church

0   10
metres

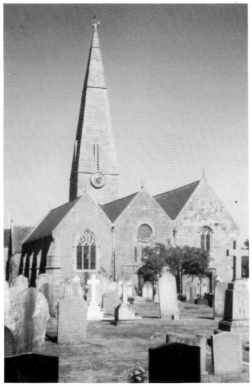

St Peter's Church   *Doorway at St Saviour's Church*

ST SAVIOUR

The south walls of the nave and chancel contain 12th century work, and the north chapel is late 13th century. Of the 15th century are the tall crossing tower, embattled with a square SW stair turret and rib-vault, the south transept now used as a vestry and the chancel east window of three lights. It appears that the original tower had a spire which collapsed onto the transept, necessitating the rebuilding of both tower and transept. The tower has three gargoyles of Chausey granite, the fourth at the SE corner having broken off. There are squinch arches to support a spire that was never built. The wide north aisle with a four bay arcade is 16th century and also of that date is the nave west wall which makes a symmetrical composition with the aisle, with doorways either side of a pair of central buttresses and diagonal buttresses on the outer corners. The SW buttress has a scallop shell and the initials G.L. thought to refer to a pilgrimage to St James of Compostella made by George Lempriere in the late 15th century, which the other buttress bears the Lempriere arms. The arcade of two round-arches between the north chapel and chancel is of later in the 16th century. The church is quite dark inside, the combined result of stripping away the plasterwork and filling the windows with stained glass. The many monuments include those to John Poingdestre, d1691, George La Cloche, d1681, and Amice La Cloche, d1725, and his wife Anne Seale, d1759. There is also a tablet to Lillie Langtry, d1929. The oldest gravestones outside go back to the 17th century.

Stalls in Trinity Church

Trinity Church

TRINITY - Holy Trinity

The lower parts of the central tower are 12th century. Of two bays, but connected by a single wide 16th century arch, are the chancel and north chapel of the second half of the 13th century. The chapel was given a new east window in the 15th century, when the north transept was rebuilt. The north windows of the chapel are 16th century. At that time a north aisle was removed and the arch to it from the transept was blocked. A wide new nave was built later, but this has been replaced by a new nave of four bays approximating to the width of the original one. In the chapel is a fine monument to Sir Edward de Carteret, d1683. On the chancel floor are slabs to Philippe Le Boutillier, d1665, Hugh Lempriere, Lord of Dielament, d1685, and Denis Guerdain, d1742, and his wife Sara Richardson, d1746.

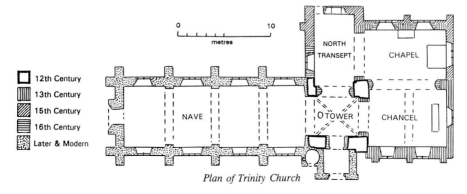

0   10
metres

☐ 12th Century
▦ 13th Century
▨ 15th Century
▤ 16th Century
▨ Later & Modern

NORTH TRANSEPT

CHAPEL

NAVE

O TOWER

CHANCEL

Plan of Trinity Church

OTHER OLD CHAPELS AND CHURCHES OF JERSEY

FISHERMEN'S CHAPEL   Parish of St Brelade

Close to the south side of St Brelade's Church is the Fisherman's Chapel, of 12th century origin, although the vault must be later and the windows have been widened (although the round-headed rere-arches look original). The name has probably arisen because of confusion over the French word pecheurs, meaning sinners or fishermen depending on which type of accent is used over the first e. The building is irregularly laid out and has a chancel with one window in each wall divided by a doubleux rising from pilasters from a nave with south and west windows, the doorway being in the NW corner. In the early 1980s excavations revealed traces of an older timber building on this site. The east wall has a 14th century wall-painting depicting the Annunciation. Used as a chantry chapel in the later medieval period, the chapel survived demolition at the Reformation by being used to house coastal artillery, the west wall being breached to allow the guns to be brought in. The building was later used as a sexton's store and then a carpenter's shop before being restored in 1883 for use as a meeting room, the west wall then being rebuilt.

HANDOIS MANOR CHAPEL   Parish of Ouen

Near the house is the low west wall of a chapel, together with part of the north wall with a doorway suggesting a 15th century date. The graveslab built into a barn opposite is thought to be that of Helier de Carteret, who colonised Sark in 1565.

Hermitage Chapel at St Helier

Fishermen's Chapel at St Brelade's

Chapel at La Hougue Bie

Chapel at La Hougue Bie

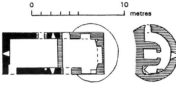

La Hougue Bie

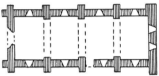

Plan of Rozel Manor Chapel

LA HOUGUE BIE   Parish of Grouville

On the summit of the ancient burial mound stand two chapels set end to end under a common roof with a belfry over the crosswall between the two. The western chapel, dedicated to Our Lady of the Dawn, is 12th century and has a west window, a SW doorway and two side-windows at the east end to light the altar. The doorway in the middle of the north side is a later insertion. The Jerusalem chapel to the east was rebuilt by Dean Richard Mabon c1520. It is vaulted like the other chapel and has doorways opposite each other at the west end, an arrangement probably to facilitate the flow of pilgrims. There are recesses in all three walls at the east end. The east end is built on a bell shaped base and contains a small room intended for a shrine. A passageway for pilgrims curves round the shrine-room from a doorway on the north side. It now has a dead end but originally steps from it rose up inside the southern recess of the chapel east end. It seems that Dean Mabon had this structure built in imitation of the nave of Holy Sepulchre at Jerusalem, a circular building with an ambulatory around a central shrine, which he had recently visited. On the vault are restored paintings of archangels bearing scrolls. They flanked a statue probably of the Assumption on a bracket with rays painted behind it on the wall. Although nothing now remains of it, a tower was built over the chapels by Philip d'Auvergue, Prince de Bouillon, who acquired the site from his uncle in 1792. The "petrified baby" then shown to visitors was probably a 16th century statue of the "Holy Babe" created for Dean Mabon's shrine room.

LONGUEVILLE MANOR CHAPEL   Parish of St Saviour

There are several late medieval references to a chapel of St Thomas Becket which stood near the dovecot erected in 1692. The chapel was sold by the Church Commissioners in 1550 and survived until the 19th century.

NOTRE DAME DE GROUVILLE   Parish of Grouville

This chapel is mentioned in 1499 as being divided from Grouville Church only by the house of Perrin le Napveu. The Church commissioners sold it in 1569 and nothing remains of it. A second chapel of St Marguerite is shown in ruins SW of the church on Plees' map of 1817. A piscina and trefoil-headed window at Grouville Court are said to be relics of it.

ROZEL MANOR - ST MARY'S CHAPEL   Parish of St Martin

In the grounds of the Lempriere seat of Rozel Manor is a vaulted chapel of four bays divided by buttresses backing onto pilasters rising to doubleux. The round-headed windows and fine west doorway date from a restoration of 1844 but the priest's doorway on the south is original. The oak choir stalls inside dating from c1600 are carved with saints, including St Bartholomew, St John, St Peter and St Thomas.

OLD BAGOT MANOR CHAPEL   Parish of St Saviour

in the Jersey Museum is what is either a piscina from this chapel or a handbasin from the manor house. One of the du Maresq family obtained a licence in 1493 for mass to be celebrated in the chapel he had recently built. Ruins of it still stood in 1802.

ST HELIER'S HERMITAGE   Parish of St Helier

This tiny vaulted chapel is built onto the site of a rock to the east of Elizabeth Castle. The north side is the natural rock and contains a recess known as St Helier's bed. A long flight of steps up from the 19th century breakwater leads up to the west doorway. There is just one tiny east window and a piscina in the SE corner. By the breakwater are slight traces of an much older oratory carved out of the rock. The 12th century priory which stood nearby is described along with Elizabeth Castle.

ST JEAN THE EVANGELIST'S CHAPEL   Parish of St Clement

Until recently walls of a chapel licensed in 1495 stood at Ivy Stone Farm.

ST MARY'S PRIORY   Parish of St Martin

Les Encrehous was given by Piers de Preaux, Lord of the Channel Islands, to the Abbey of Val Richer in Normandy, which then established a priory on the islet. In 1309 the prior stated that he, one other monk, and a servant lived in the priory and kept a light burning there to warn shipping away from the dangerous reef. Excavations in 1928 revealed traces of a chapel 3m wide by 5m long internally with a piscina, two east windows and one south window. The west doorway opened towards the living quarters, a building 8m long continuing the line of the chapel.

Several other medieval chapels existed on Jersey but have vanished without trace. The chapel at St Ouen's Manor is described along with the manor house on page 53. There were leper houses with chapels dedicated to St Nicholas on the hill opposite Mont Orgueil Castle and near Oak Walk at Carrefour St Nicholas.

OTHER CHANNEL ISLANDS FORTS AND CHURCHES

ALDERNEY

Incorporated into one corner of a large 19th century fort above Longny Bay, now converted into flats after use as a hospital, is a fragment of a fort begun in 1546, left unfinished in 1553, and later referred to as Essex Castle. The original fort was designed to have corner bastions and a central building with angle turrets. There are many other 19th century forts on Alderney. A fort probably of Roman date called the Nunnery at the head of Longny Bay has solid bastions projecting from the rounded corners. The walls are up to 1.5m thick and 5m high. A later wall cuts off the collapsed SE corner. The gunports probably date from when the fort was armed with cannon in 1540, although it is described as a blockhouse in 1435. The Chamberlayne family inhabited this building after being granted Alderney by Elizabeth I in 1584. It was used as a barracks in the 18th century and saw further use in the 1940s.

Nothing survives of the medieval church of the principal settlement at St Anne's, nor of the aisle and chapel added to it by Henri Le Mesurier in 1761. The surviving clock tower of 1767 seems to have stood in an unusual position at the east end, possibly replacing the medieval chancel. Until the late 17th century the church was dedicated to St Mary. The heavily buttressed medieval nave was replaced in 1847-50 by a new church designed by George Gilbert Scott for Canon John Le Mesurier.

A chapel of St Michel stood by the Stranger's Cemetery at Les Rochers, and another perhaps stood by the spring at L'Essource near Rose Farmand there was a chapel of St Aichadrius near La Pierre de Vilaine. There is also mention of a chapel of St Clair and of others to St Barbe and St Nicholas, although these could have been chapels flanking the chancel of the medieval parish church.

HERM

Close to the Manor House stands a vaulted 13th century chapel St Tugual with a north chapel. It belonged to the Augustinian Abbey at Cherbourg until they were dispossessed in 1413. From the 1440s the chapel seems to have been served by the Franciscans at St Peter Port. They added the house to the east end of the chapel.

SARK

Above the narrow isthmus that joins Little Sark to the mainland is a star-shaped earthwork fort attributed by locals to the time of the French invasion of 1549 and refortified by the Germans in the 1940s. On the main island is a refuge called Le Fort partly enclosed by a rampart and water-filled ditch. Above the old landing place at Eperquerie is the site of an artillery battery of the 17th or 18th century. The church of St Peter has a nave and tower (later heightened) of 1820 and a chancel of 1880.

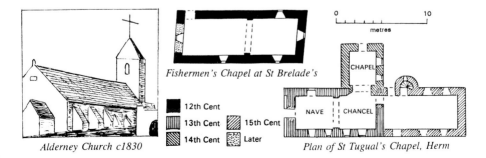

Fishermen's Chapel at St Brelade's

■ 12th Cent
▥ 13th Cent ▨ 15th Cent
▧ 14th Cent ▒ Later

Alderney Church c1830

CHAPEL

NAVE CHANCEL

0   10
metres

Plan of St Tugual's Chapel, Herm

GLOSSARY OF ARCHITECTURAL TERMS

Ashlar - Masonry of blocks with even faces and square edges.
Bailey - Defensible court enclosed by a wall or a palisade and ditch.
Barbican - Defensible court, passage or porch in front of an entrance.
Baroque - A whimsical and odd form of the Classical architectural style.
Bastion - A projection rising no higher than the curtain wall it flanks.
Broaches - Sloping half pyramids adapting an octagonal spire to a square tower.
Casemate - A room within a thick wall of a fortification.
Chancel - The eastern part of a church used by the clergy.
Clerestory - An upper storey pierced by windows lighting the floor below.
Corbel - A projecting bracket to support other stonework of a timber beam.
Credence Shelf - She,lf or niche for the Eucharistic elements before consecration.
Crossing Tower - A tower built on four arches in the middle of a cruciform church.
Cruciform Church - A cross-shaped church with transepts forming the arms of the cross.
Curtain Wall - A high enclosing stone wall around a bailey.
Cusp - A projecting point between the foils of a foiled Gothic arch.
Dado - The decorative covering of the lower part of a wall or screen.
Demi-Bastion - A bastion just one side of an enciente instead of two.
Doubleux - A thin strip like a pilaster (and sometimes rising from one) on a vault.
Easter Sepulchre - A recess in a chancel which received an effigy of Christ at Easter.
Flamboyant - The latest phase of French Gothic with wavy undulating lines in tracery.
Floriated - Decorated with flower or leaf-like forms.
Foil - A lobe formed by the cusping of a circle or arch.
Gunport - An embrasure suitable for the discharge of heavy cannon.
Hoodmould - A projecting moulding above a lintel or arch to throw off water.
Impost - A wall bracket, often moulded, to support one end of an arch.
Jamb - The side of a doorway, window, or other opening.
Keep - A tower or enclosure acting as a citadel or ultimate strongpoint.
Lancet - A long and comparatively narrow window with a pointed head.
Light - A compartment of a window.
Lintel - A horizontal stone or beam spanning an opening.
Lucarne - Very narrow opening, especially upon a tower or spire.
Loop - A small opening to admit light or for the discharge of missiles.
Machicolation - A slot for dropping or firing missiles down upon assailants.
Martello Tower - Early 19th century coastal defence tower, usually circular.
Moat - A defensive ditch, water filled or dry bottomed.
Moellon - A small roughly shaped block.
Mullion - A vertical member dividing the lights of a window.
Nave - The part of a church in which the congregation sits or stands.
Nook-shaft - A column set in the angle of a pier or respond or jamb of an opening.
Norman - A division of English Romanesque architecture from 1066 to 1200.
Ogival Arch - Arch of oriental origin with both convex and concave curves.
Parapet - A wall for protection at any sudden drop.
Pilaster - Flat buttress or pier attached to a wall.
Piscina - A stone basin used for rinsing out holy vessels after a mass.
Portcullis - A wooden gate made to rise and fall in vertical grooves.
Postern - A back entrance or lesser gateway.
Quoins - Dressed stones at the corners of a building.
Rere-Arch - An arch on the inside face of a window embrasure or doorway.
Respond - A half pier or column bonded into a wall and carrying an arch.
Reticulation - Tracery with a net-like appearence.
Ringwork - A embanked enclosure of more modest size than a bailey.
Sedilia - Seats for clergy (usually three) in the south wall of a chancel.
Saddle-Back Roof - A steep sided gabled roof, sometimes used upon church towers.
Tracery - Intersecting ribwork in the upper part of a later Gothic window.
Trefoil - A three lobed section of tracery.
Voussoir - Wedge-shaped stone forming part of an arch.
Wall-Walk - A walkway on top of a wall, always protected by a parapet.
Ward - A stone walled defensive enclosure.